PRAISE FO

"To achieve greatness, you must have a purpose and a fire burning within. Cardiff has taken his passion to helping individuals and created a guide anyone can follow in *Tide Turners*. Follow his guidance and prepare to IGNITE!"

John Lee Dumas of EOFire

"Cardiff has been a continuous learner and it shows in *Tide Turners*. He has taken what he has learned, and then applied it to his own life as well as craft a wonderful guide for anyone to follow."

Ray Higdon, Best Selling Author and Founder of Top Earner Academy and The 3-Minute Expert

"You'll find the momentum you need for positive change inside the pages of *Tide Turners*. Author Cardiff Hall sets you on a clear path toward sustaining high achievement."

Kary Oberbrunner, author of *ELIXIR Project, Day Job to Dream Job, The Deeper Path*, and *Your Secret Name*

"If you indeed want to gain control of your life while tapping into the purpose you want to live out, then *Tide Turners* is the book for you. Cardiff has provided a solid layout to prepare you for a successful life, while doing so in a relatable manner!"

Kenny Pugh, Entrepreneur Life Coach

"Cardiff has a tremendous impact on every person he meets. His friendship, intellect, and zest for life is unparalleled. His tenacity, commitment to his work, and infectious enthusiasm causes everyone in his life to rise up with him! For those of you who do not know him personally, you now can benefit from his knowledge by reading his new book, *Tide Turners*! This is a must read. Enjoy and be lifted."

Ed Ennis, Public Speaker and Entrepreneur

"Sometimes 'control' seems so out of reach but it can be found. You can absolutely harness the power that you have within your heart to drive purposefully in the direction of your greatest dreams and desires. Cardiff shares real life examples and meaningful stories that illuminate key points in a way that allows you to naturally see your path through this practical guide to sustained achievement and greater joy in your life."

Felicia Mupo, Entrepreneur, Home-based Business

"Everything happens perfectly in life. If you continually think something negative is happening TO YOU instead of just happening in life, it will always kill your attitude and happiness. Cardiff's amazing positive nature and relentless pursuit of helping others has created an amazing book to allow you to reach an untouchable level of greatness!"

Terry Gremaux, CEO of Independent Sales Agency

"The power to have control of where your life is heading does exist, and *Tide Turners* is the book which amplifies how you can do just that. Cardiff delivers a common sense approach anyone can do and implement."

Jim Akers, author of *Tape Breakers*

"Cardiff is an encourager! The book reads like a series of encouraging messages to you to keep going and not give up. Cardiff is honest about his own journey and provides practical guidance to stay the course."

Kyle Robinson, Pastor at Wooddale-Edina Church

"If you feel like you are drifting in life and desire more, this book is the perfect tool to begin the journey and take control. Cardiff shows us how this can be done by taking you on a journey with the exact map."

Mark LaMaster, author of
Friday Night Lights for Fathers and Sons

Tide
TURNERS

Tide TURNERS

The Practical Guide to Help You Feel in Control, Experience More Joy, and Sustain Achievement in Life

CARDIFF D. HALL

AUTHOR ACADEMY elite

Published by Author Academy Elite
P.O. Box 43, Powell, OH 43035
www.AuthorAcademyElite.com

Paperback ISBN- 978-1-943526-45-1
Hardcover ISBN- 978-1-943526-44-4

Library of Congress Control Number: 2016909285

Illustrations by Rahul Bajad

For my wife Dawn and my daughter Molly,

Light of my world.

Thanks for allowing me the time away from you

To bring this book to life.

CONTENTS

"No matter your position, circumstances, or opportunities in life, you always have the freedom of mind to choose how you experience, interpret, and ultimately shape your world."

Brendon Burchard

FOREWORD

Have you fallen off the self-improvement wagon one too many times and come to believe that the kind of success you dream about is out of reach?

Are your good intentions easily overcome by your lack of self-discipline?

Do you ever feel you "just don't have what it takes" to win at life?

Do many self-help authors come across to you as hopeless overachievers with whom you have a difficult time relating?

Do you want to improve your life without having to read a 300-page book in order to learn how?

Have you ever read a book with lots of great information but didn't know how to translate it into a simple, daily plan for life-changing experiences?

Have you been turned off by self-help gurus whose real goal seems to be turning you into an ongoing revenue stream for their business empires?

If you've been searching for a book that offers practical and yet life-changing lessons and tips anyone can adopt, using a simple daily plan that won't take twenty hours to read, and written by an author who shares wisdom gained from living with the same struggles we all have, then this book is for you.

In these pages you will learn simple but profound lessons for daily living, such as:

- Why failure is a good thing
- How anyone can master commitment through a simple process
- How to consistently overcome the unexpected without being taken off course

I've known Cardiff Hall for almost 15 years and can tell you that he's a regular person, just like you and me. He's had to learn the principles he shares in this book, one at a time. He's worked to overcome some of the same tendencies most of us have in common, such as enjoying a little extra sleep in the morning instead of harnessing that time for something better.

Over the years I've watched as he has gained the experience he writes about in these pages. He has tried lots of different things in the business and personal areas of his life. I have seen him pursue ideas that came to a dead end, and experience excitement over new ideas as well as disappointment when a plan didn't work out the way he intended.

The wisdom in this book is from a guy who has made his way through life with the same limitations we all have, such as family and a job. He's not a professional self-help guru. Cardiff has learned how to succeed by trial and error. He knows that success isn't a destination, it's a journey—one that can be undertaken by anyone with the same amount of willpower and focus we all possess.

I've spent many, many hours with Cardiff, answering questions and exchanging ideas. He's sharing his lessons in this book so that you won't have to learn them the way that he did, and to give you a head start. He's figured it out, so you don't have to. If you ever have the privilege of getting to know Cardiff, you'll come to realize that's just the sort of person he is. One of his most attractive characteristics is that he's all about YOU.

If you only take away one thing from this introduction, let it be this: YOU CAN DO THE THINGS IN THIS BOOK.

It won't take a Herculean level of commitment or self-discipline. It's also not an "all-or-nothing" proposition: you won't have to adopt everything in these pages in order to see life-changing improvements.

As Cardiff says, a concept or change that takes you a single second to adopt can have a profoundly positive effect on the rest of your life. Because Cardiff is an ordinary guy who didn't start out with advantages that most of us don't have, such as wealth or an Ivy League education, ordinary people like you and me can use the simple and yet profound strategies in this book to succeed far beyond what we ever thought possible.

So read on and enjoy the journey with Cardiff, as I have had the opportunity to do.

Mark Summers
Chief Executive Officer and President
ThreeWire

Note to the Reader
TIDE TURNERS DEFINITION

Turn the tide is an expression often used when someone causes a reversal in the direction of events. That's the standard definition. If true, then it should stand to reason that those with the capacity to turn the tides would be dubbed Tide Turners.

Tide Turners are individuals or a group that are purposeful in their actions, taking great efforts toward achievement with an unrelenting will, desire, and commitment to succeed — regardless of what lies ahead.

Tide Turners typically share many of the same characteristics:
- Steadfast belief in oneself
- Are optimistic in the midst of fear
- Courageous in the face of adversity
- Are committed to growth
- Devotion to a personal cause
- Network of advocates and supporters
- Foresight to see failures as opportunities to learn and grow
- Push for greatness within themselves
- Understand where they want to go or achieve
- Have a passion to win

Some examples of current and past Tide Turners (*this includes a few of my personal favorites*):

Steve Jobs – Revolutionized technology.

Harriet Tubman – Risked her life to help individuals escape slavery.[1]

Martin Luther King – Changed the history on race equality in America.

2014 National Championship Football Team – The Ohio State Buckeyes, resilience to play through adversity.

Erica McCuen – The story of her sorrow, pain, and going beyond her comfort zone is shared in this book.

Alice Coachman – First black female to win a gold medal in the 1948 Olympics.[2]

Oprah Winfrey –Transcended a difficult childhood and rose to the heights of success.[3]

University of Connecticut Women's Basketball Team – Winners of 11 National Championships.[4]

Darci Olson - Her amazing weight loss story is shared in this book.

Coach John Wooden – Inspirational coach and leader of seven consecutive national championships.[5]

You _____
(Enter Your Name Here)

Tide Turners do not compare themselves to anyone and nor should you. You possess the ability within you to be a TIDE TURNER!

Access your free Tide Turners bonus materials at www.cardiffdhall.com/resources.

INTRODUCTION
WAVES CAUSE MOVEMENT

"If you could go anywhere, where you like to go? Not in terms of vacations, but in your life. You see, we're all on a journey, whether we know it or not. We are traveling inevitably toward the ends of our lives. So the real question for us is whether we're going to select a destination and steer a course for it, or allow ourselves to be swept along with the tide, letting others determine where we'll end up. The choice is entirely up to us."[1]

John C. Maxwell

The alarm goes off. You decide to hit the snooze button on your phone or clock. You whisper to yourself, "Just one more snooze." The time goes by quickly, and again the alarm goes off. Your hand makes the motion to hit the snooze but something in your head tells you, "It's time." Again, you mumble and turn your alarm off, staring at the ceiling, at the side of the room or perhaps at your pillow. Maybe you don't even need an alarm and something else is calling, and it's the bathroom. Can you relate to this? I know I did. I would hit the snooze—well, let's just say if there was a limit on the snooze I'd reach it.

Rubbing your eyes to erase the overnight fog, your feet hit the floor and the day officially begins. Unbeknownst to you, you are about to enter a wave. You may be thinking, "I'm in my house getting ready for the day, and you're telling me I'm about to enter a wave." Yes, everyone enters waves and the wave of the day is different for everyone.

Waves occur in different sizes, shapes, and strengths. Some waves are so subtle you completely miss them—they don't impact you; however, they do eventually impact you. There are big waves, the massive ones that toss you around, and you don't even see them coming. Imagine you are in Hawaii and you see the biggest wave a surfer is riding, leaving you completely amazed. Then suddenly, the rider is gone. The wave has taken the rider down. That is exactly what a wave can do to you.

Each day when waves occur, everyone handles them differently. There are only two ways a wave can be handled: positively or negatively. While being tossed around by a powerful wave is painful, your reaction to that wave will tell much about yourself.

A wave is an invisible force that has a sizable impact within oneself, which, over time, ultimately shapes the course of your life.

In this book, I share personal stories of my own waves that had the impact only a wave could make. Some would say these are life lessons; however, a life lesson is only made if you decide to understand it and make positive changes to your course. Have you ever had that wave that capsizes your 'boat'? I share a personal story that did that for me.

Throughout the pages, you will be exposed to 15 different waves. Going through each wave, it's my ultimate goal for you to feel in control of that wave, and in doing so, your journey will offer purpose, joy, and a rich blessed life. There will be practical principles shared that if implemented will allow you to feel in control of your life.

I've had the opportunity to invest in courses and books, and attend conferences to help build up my internal power so I can be in control of my journey in life. Today, when the alarm goes off or when the bathroom calls, I have this sense of purpose—and I want the same for you.

Now, do I hit the snooze button?

Yes, at times, though there is this calling within my mind that tells me to "take the step bravely toward the day with excitement and a feeling of control."

The waves expressed throughout the chapters include sports. I enjoy sports and share stories of athletes, coaches, and events that illustrate meaning.

The waves of life can be powerful and overtake you, but this book can help navigate these waves.

Do you have your life jacket on? Did you get one with the book? Unfortunately, my publisher, Author Academy Elite, wouldn't attach one to the book. That's ok. I have mine on and so do you—you are holding it. Are you ready to jump into the waves? Get ready to go through each wave and then know with certainty that you can begin to take control of your ship.

Visit the following link to get your free access to the Tide Turners bonus material now:

www.cardiffdhall.com/resources

PART 1
LOST AT SEA

CHAPTER 1
THE WAVE OF THE CIRCLE

A CONTINUOUS LOOP WITH
NO UPWARD MOTION

Some call the loop the hamster wheel. You've seen the hamster wheel, right? The little furry creature spends time moving the wheel in the same motion, never truly going anywhere and does it for hours. Have you ever found yourself in the loop? I know I have.

The Loop Defined

The loop consists of waking up, getting ready for the day, going to work, spending family time, sitting in front of the TV or social media to "veg out," go to bed, and then I believe you know what happens next. The loop continues. For many the loop is tiring. Just like the hamster who has to take some breaks, you too must stop momentarily and then return to enter the loop once again.

Albert Einstein stated it every so profoundly, *"Insanity is doing the same thing over and over again and expecting different results."*

When I was in the loop, it hadn't seemed like insanity, but I knew something was missing. Perhaps right now you are in the loop, and just doing what you know needs to be done is exhausting. You know deep inside that there must be more.

Have you ever heard of this? "If you get your education, get a good job, get married, and retire, then you have lived a good life." But today, you ask yourself. Is this it? Is this what life is meant to be? Me living in this loop and doing the same day after day, after day?

Living in the loop doesn't allow for any upward movement or growth. It cannot scientifically impact your life. There are times you could think that each day is different. However, the motion going around the loop is the same.

Every year, on February 2, there is a special day in Punxsutawney, Pennsylvania called Groundhog's Day. On this day a groundhog called Punxsutawney Phil comes out of hibernation so he can look for his shadow. If Phil sees his shadow, it's regarded as an omen of six more weeks of winter, and Phil goes back into hibernation for six more weeks. On the other hand, if Phil does not see a shadow, it is a sign that spring is coming, and Phil breaks his hibernation.

Living in a loop is like hibernation; it's the same day after day until one day you have an awakening. On this day you step out of the loop to see if things can be different today. For some of you, you will just head right back into hibernation while others decide to stay out and see how things could change.

Remember the hamster? To get the hamster out of the loop, someone needs to pick them up and remove them from the area and let them roam around and explore. The loop has to be broken to change the outcome.

The Loop Can Be Broken

The loop can be broken when a life-changing event happens or you become self-aware and make a decision to break out of the loop. Later in this book I'll discuss how this happened to me. I wanted to give you a sample of the questions that can help you break out of the loop, which can be found in the Tide Tuners free resource, available for free download at www.cardiffdhall.com/resources.

"How do I feel about my life?"
"Do I feel stuck within a loop?"
"Am I responsible for where I am today in my life?"

Answering these questions and others' questions can help you become aware.

Know you can break out of your loop, but first you must be aware that you are in a loop. Once you become self-aware there are actions that must be taken. The hamster couldn't remove themselves from their little home; however when someone else did it, they got off the loop. You too can get out of the loop but you need help. The only person who can impact this move is YOU. You must decide to take the necessary actions and step out of the loop so there can be upward movement and exploration.

Just a few years ago, I found myself in this very same the loop. Doing things day after day with no intent of breaking the routine. Now don't get me wrong, the loop can be enjoyable since you know what to expect every day. It becomes the norm and a place of safety and comfort. Do you have a favorite couch or chair you sit in? I do, and I can just imagine the feeling and comfort of that chair, ahhhh. That's what the loop can feel like at times.

If I think back to my childhood, I was the one who'd say I can do something, and then I would do it. It's funny how when you think of it, the loop doesn't come along until later in life. Kids aren't in a loop, they are carefree. They dream of things they want to do and explore. There is this daily wonderment that kids take each day. As we progress through life, we move from the wonderment path toward the loop of life—with the demands of a job, family, and activities—until eventually, we get stuck in the loop.

Having been stuck in the loop, I had to ask myself some difficult questions, which has taken me along a new journey and has allowed me to break out of the loop. Remember that favorite couch or chair? When you break out of the loop at first, you will most likely not feel the nice comfort you have been enjoying. Think about it. You've been in the loop for a long time, doing the same thing day after day, and when the loop breaks all of a sudden you experience CHANGE! Your body and mind get a shock. Something is different, and your body wants to get you back in the loop.

When I finally decided to break the loop, my body and mind noticed something was different. But I wasn't pulled back into the loop this time and my life really changed. That can also happen to you.

Do you want to know how you can do that for yourself? I know you do! The loop is controlling; it steals away dreams, ideas, ambition, motivation, joy, and true happiness. You've got to get off the loop to have a better life.

Personal Loop Break - Failed Attempt

There was a point earlier in my life when I attempted my first loop break. The household I grew up in focused on getting an education. My dad was a principal and teacher, and education was important in our home. If I messed up at school, my dad would find out before I came home. I made all of school a priority and set my goal to attend the one college that I desired. I wanted to attend Ohio State University and be a BUCKEYE. As I was growing up, my father obtained another degree. The path was set for me to follow in his footsteps. I went through undergrad business school and the MBA was looming for me. I've always heard you needed your MBA to have an opportunity to advance in your career. However, I did not pursue the MBA immediately after graduation.

Instead, I worked five years at a large consumer goods company and got in the loop. My job became routine and I was going through the motions. I decided to study for the GMAT and get my MBA from one of the best business management schools. I knew this would be the "thing" that would allow me to break out of the loop.

After many hours of studying, the big day for the GMAT at the University of Minnesota arrived. I still remember it to this day. The walk, where I parked and how I felt going through the test. I felt nervous and apprehensive, yet I wanted to prevail. Have you ever put so much effort into something and when the day came to perform, it didn't feel right? It was a long day. After the GMAT I began the application process to several schools.

If you have ever applied to business schools, you know it can be a lengthy process. I enjoyed the process of being personally interviewed at each school, talking one on one and sharing why I felt my presence in the program would benefit me and the school.

Have you ever waited for news that came in the regular postal mail? Have you ever waited for that letter that informs you of a decision? Well, I waited and checked my mailbox every day. Today, business schools probably email you or post the letter on a secure site telling you if you have been selected or not to their program. But I had to wait for the letters to arrive in the mail. The first letter that came started something like this.

> *"Dear Mr. Hall, we are writing to inform you that while your qualifications are good and you interviewed well, we felt there are other candidates who meet our criteria, and thus your application has been denied. We wish you the best of luck in your future endeavor."*

I was disappointed but not distraught. I knew a second letter was coming. The day arrived, and again there was a similar tone to the letter: "We wish you the best of luck in your future endeavors."

The Loop Can Reappear

Disappointed from the letters and disappointed in myself given I attempted to make the leap and get off my loop, I was pulled right back in easily. Can you recall a certain moment in your life when you attempted to make that leap but it didn't go as planned?

What I didn't realize was a different plan was in store for me, a plan that would allow me to move into a different organization within the company. When I look back upon that experience, what I thought was going to be the way to break the loop became something else entirely.

Through that experience of being rejected from graduate schools, which some would say was a "failure," I kept my positive attitude.

Life can often be just like what I have experienced. You attempt to make that loop leap but it just doesn't go like you'd hoped. However, there is one thing only you can control and that is how you will react. Even though you may not understand why something is happening the way it is, you can decide to stay positive and believe that everything will turn out for the best.

The Loop Choice

The loop can be broken. But it is a choice. Even if you have attempted and failed before, you should never give up hope.

While I did move out of the loop I was in, over time I eventually fell right back into the loop. Once you leave the loop, it doesn't mean you are clear of the loop for life. It takes a well-navigated course not to be pulled back in. Have you ever lost weight only to gain it back? The same can happen when you leave the loop unless it's directly tied to a well-defined, focused, and highly navigated course, which we will discuss in the next chapter.

The continuous loop is broken for good once you have that defined course as your foundation. You can support that course in other ways, and we will delve more into this in later chapters.

"You can't build a great building on a weak foundation. You must have a solid foundation if you're going to have a strong superstructure."

Gordon B. Hinckley

You can build that strong foundation and it starts with your VISION.

Key Points

1. The loop consists of the same daily motion, day after day.
2. Doing the same thing over and over with no results and expecting change is like trying to remove the salt from the ocean.
3. The loop is not always permanent; it can be broken.
4. Becoming self-aware by acknowledging you are in a loop is the first step to breaking the loop.
5. Your attitude is controllable.
6. You can be pulled back into the loop by not having a defined course.
7. Departure from the loop requires a strong foundation.

CHAPTER 2
THE WAVE OF FLOATING
CREATE YOUR VISION

I have been in the loop myself and when I really think about it, I realize I was lost at sea. I was floating and allowing the tide to take me wherever it flowed. Have you ever watched a tree branch flow down a river or stream with the tide? The branch flows with the tide and gets caught on something, stopping its movement. Then when something hits the branch, maybe a strong tide, it gets released. The branch begins to flow again, this time spinning around due to the strong tide. With the tide controlling its direction, the branch finally gets slammed against a big stack of other branches, stuck, and its journey is over.

Floating – The act of not owning up to the fact that you ultimately have the responsibility for your life, and by not taking responsibility, your life is tossed about by the direction of the tide.

The Wave Takes You Wherever It Wants

Remember my first attempt at breaking the loop? I left the dock feeling great about my new position, yet I didn't plan out my course. I just went with the wave. The wind that controls the wave blows on all of us; however, unless we set the sails to be in control, we allow the wave to take us wherever it flows.

Have you ever thought about why some people just allow the wind to blow them about, never truly taking control? If not, that is ok. I didn't either. I thought that was part of life. You go through it and that is the way it's supposed to be. Now recalling that statement, "If you get your education, get a good job, get _____." Yes, you probably can recite it by now. That philosophy is what I thought I was supposed to do.

> *"The pessimist complains about the wind; the optimist expects it to change; the realist adjusts the sails."*

> William Arthur Ward

That quote stings a bit. Here I was being the optimist hoping the winds would change, which was something I just expected. And you might feel the same way. When I look within, I realize I had felt this way. It didn't make me sad or depressed. It was just what I felt was normal. It was my philosophy until I heard a question that altered my thinking.

The Question That Can Alter Your Course

When I heard successful entrepreneur Ray Higdon ask a group, "Do you have a vision?" I responded as someone who had been in Corporate America for many years. My thoughts went to the pictures and bulletin boards plastered all around my workplace about the company and where the company was going.

A vision, defined in the business dictionary, is: *An aspirational description of what an organization would like to achieve or accomplish in the mid-term or long term future. It is intended to serves as a clear guide for choosing current and future courses of action.*[1]

The company had outlined its future, the values it stood for, and the upward movement toward growing a larger business. Never did I realize, until that moment, that individuals could also have a vision. I thought that was only for organizations.

A personal vision defined for you is replacing organization with the word "you." See below.

An aspirational description of what you *would like to achieve or accomplish in the mid-term or long term future. It is intended to serves as a clear guide for choosing current and future courses of action.*

So, naturally, my answer to Ray's question was, "No, I do not have a vision for my life."

Up until then, I was going through life, accepting things because that was just the way it was. My life went where the wind was blowing.

Craft a Vision for Your Life

No one taught me about crafting a vision while I was at Ohio State University. What I came to realize in my group training with Ray was that to truly succeed at something, a vision must be crafted. As we walk through life, a very high percentage of us do not have a vision. If you are not creating a vision for yourself, someone else will create it for you. When I came upon what Grant Cardone quoted in his book, *The 10X Rule*, what he said truly hit me squarely in the head. I trust it will do the same for you.

"As long as you live, you will either accomplish your own goals and dreams OR will be used as a resource to accomplish the goals and dreams of others."

Grant Cardone

Did that quote hurt a bit? It hurt when I read it. It made me realize I had to do something and that would have to start with a vision. When Ray asked that question I became fully aware in that moment. I was being a resource to accomplish other people's goals and dreams, yet I had my own goals and dreams but didn't have a vision.

A vision starts with the end in mind and is crafted in writing. The power of taking pen to paper and crafting out your vision is the first step to release you from floating in the wave. Here are just a few examples of questions you need to answer.

- Fulfillment – What is it you truly want?
- Direction – Where do you want to take your life?
- Passion – What is it that you want to do?
- Legacy – What do you want to be known for?
- What steps do you need to take for all of these goals to be fulfilled?

The answers to these questions are the foundation of crafting your vision for your life. In the bonus materials you will have the opportunity to craft your personal vision. You can access these materials at www.cardiffdhall.com/resources.

"As humans we hunger for a vision. If we are unable to create a compelling vision for ourselves, we will latch on to someone else's vision. With no vision for our future, we extinguish our powerful internal fire!"

Ray Higdon

This quote is powerful. Many people do not have a vision and they allow the winds to toss and turn them, and then they complain about their circumstances. You must realize you can choose to create a vision for your life.

Time for Action

Have you taken the time to write down your answers to the five questions above? I hope you said YES!! If not, what are you waiting for? Perhaps you are waiting until you reach the end of the book. Why? The words aren't going anywhere, they will still be here.

When Ray asked that question and after the class ended, I knew I had to take action. The next morning, I sat at my desk and asked myself these questions plus more. I took my pen and wrote out answers, and drafted the vision I wanted. Not someone else's vision, but mine. You can do the same. Will you take the time right now to do this process? Your ability for action or inaction will determine much in your life.

When you complete the answers to those questions, see yourself like a director shooting a film. Mentally snap pictures of yourself. For example, imagine that you wanted to take more family vacations. Frame pictures within your mind and see the fulfillment of your vision for more vacations.

- What are you doing on your vacation?
- Where is the vacation?
- How are the looks on the faces of your family members when you take a vacation you have talked about for years?
- How does it feel when you first arrive at your vacation destination?

Start to mentally paint a picture with great clarity and see your vacation in high definition picture quality, and your entire future in the same way. After you have decided what you want and you have attached the details and feelings, think about what is "the benefit of the benefit," a concept discussed by Ray Higdon.

Let me explain about "the benefit of the benefit." Stick with the vision of taking the ultimate vacation with your family. After that vacation, what was the benefit? Perhaps it is just getting away from your job to relax, and the benefit of the benefit is that you get to spend time with your family and bond with them. You enjoy the fun and laughter together while recharging your soul, so you can excel at your job when you return.

Now that you understand the benefit of the benefit, you must associate feelings with your vision.

- How will it feel?
- What will you experience?

Giving your vision feelings gives your vision life. Individuals act on emotion. Your vision needs to have a feeling and be driven by emotion, so your body will take action to continue towards your vision.

When writing your vision, you may have already incorporated emotion into your vision; however, it is important to make sure you include the feelings you will experience.

Using the vacation vision, what are the feelings you will have upon arrival of your destination? Gratitude? Blessedness? Hunger after a long trip? Accomplished for having done it? Excitement? Peace? Feel those feelings in your body and also put them down on paper.

It is also important to think about how others will view your attainment of that vision.

- What will their reaction be to your planned vacation?
- Will there be jealousy, happiness, and/or stunned feelings by others?
- What will be the expressions on their faces?
- What will their comments be on social media updates about your vacation?

Begin to see all of that and feel it. Attaching feelings to your vision will provide the catalyst for you to continue on your path of achieving your vision.

"Feeling the details of that vision will pull you past the point of quitting."

Ray Higdon

Imprint Your Vision Within Your Mind Daily

With a vision crafted and your feelings attached to them, the next step is using affirmations and questions. Write down this statement, "I am so happy and grateful that _____." Insert your vision. You want to repeat this aloud and say the affirmation every day. I recommend you state this at minimum twice per day—first thing when you wake up and right before you go to bed. You can also enter it as a reminder on your phone. I do this and have my phone remind me three times per day. Creating triggers like this will enable you to have that mental shift within your subconscious mind, which will help you achieve your vision.

For each affirmation, ask yourself:

- Why am I so happy and grateful that I _____?
- How will I feel when I am so happy and grateful I _____?
- What do I need to do, so I am so happy and grateful I_____?

Achieving your vision does not just happen by stating an affirmation or reading it on your phone. It does require action on your part. Affirmation and action work together to help you achieve.

Your vision is the rudder for your life, and if you use the rudder, you will experience a life that is full. Although your life may not be easy, you can feel assured that the ending point will be a life of fulfillment and not of regret.

Key Points

1. The wave will take you wherever it wants unless you decide to take control.
2. Companies create a vision for their future and you must also create your own personal vision to set the course for your life.
3. Your vision is crafted by answering questions.
4. Make sure your vision contains feelings so it is connected to your heart's desire.
5. Create triggers throughout the day that will remind you of your personally crafted vision and allow it to be absorbed into your mind.
6. Your set vision will act as your lighthouse that pulls you through the point of quitting.
7. You have permission to create your own vision, which enables you to set the desired course for your life.

PART 2
DOCKING

CHAPTER 3
THE WAVE OF THE
UNPLANNED EVENT

THE STOPPING MOMENT

Have you ever had the "stopping" moment occur? The moment you didn't expect, didn't really plan for where you find yourself right in the eye of the hurricane. Hurricanes can cause significant disaster and their path of destruction can often be felt for miles.

Hurricane Katrina, which occurred on August 23rd, 2005, had great impact on all those in New Orleans. Perhaps you know many of those affected, or perhaps you were living in that area when Katrina hit. That moment changed everything for those involved, and there will be moments like this in your own life.

Every day, twenty-four hours a day, seven days a week, something is always happening. There may be calm, peace, busyness, or fullness. There is always something occurring and it does not always have to be bad.

Do you ever wonder why you cannot just "pause" your life?

Many people would love to "pause" their life. Perhaps they do not want to face an upcoming event, or perhaps an event is so joyful they just want to hold it, or perhaps they just need a break from whatever is happening.

However, your life does not have a pause button. It continues to move regardless of whether you want it to or not. Keep in mind that how you choose to handle these moments will determine your outcome in life.

"When a defining moment comes along, you can do one of two things. Define the moment or let the moment define you."

Kevin Costner, from the film *Tin Cup*

The Event

When I was working for a packaged goods company, I had a life event occur where I could not reach for that pause. I clearly remember the event. It is etched in my mind. One Thursday, in the spring of 2006, my wife mentioned there was a large deposit from my company that was showing up in our bank account. It was not bonus time and I clearly did not understand why there would be a large deposit in my account. I just thought the company made some kind of mistake. I went to sleep thinking the company made a mistake and I would contact payroll, who would then take care of it.

Once I arrived in the office, there were two individuals waiting for me. The first was my manager who had flown in from Chicago. The other was from Human Resource, and she had flown in from Columbus. My head quickly began to hurt and my heart sank. I asked myself, "Why is this happening to me, and why did they both fly in to see me at 8 AM?" We sat in the conference room and papers were shoved into my hands, indicating it was my last day of employment. The manager said, "We are moving in a different direction and today is your last day. You are to pack your office personal belongings and not touch your computer. I will drive you home, and you will no longer have a car."

This life event just punched me in the stomach so hard I could not even breathe. I could not understand why this was happening to me. I had just won a trip to Maui with the company, and yet, today I was being told to leave. I was numb. I remember packing up the office and my manager driving the car home while I told him the directions to my house. I was home by 8:45 AM that Friday.

It was a serious blow not having a car, which had been provided by my employer, and facing the lack of a steady paycheck. I had not expected or planned this life event. Stunned, I could not believe this had actually happened to me, even when reality sank in. I could not eat, and my eyes blurred from the tears streaming down my face. I kept saying over and over, "Why me, why me?" I did not have the nerve to call my wife. I just sat on the couch in a trance all day, finally lying down in the darkness as evening came.

Action Taken for Healing

This life event wound was deep, and I only knew one way to allow it to heal. I could not take pity on myself or blame anyone. I had to take action. The following Monday I attended a job transition meeting at my church, and the healing began. I made a choice about how I was going to face this unexpected event, although I had no idea what the next week, month, or future held for my wife and me.

When you go through something unexpected you have a choice about everything. This includes your attitude, your desire, your feelings, your mindset, and how you want to manage the event. You have a choice, and only you can decide. I made the decision to face the event head on and my focus was on a solution. *"How can I get a job as quickly as possible so I can contribute to the financial needs of my family?"*

Instead of feeling sorry for myself, I chose to have a great attitude, but I knew it would be hard work to find a new job. I also knew that having the right attitude and approach would help me move through this unexpected and unpleasant event quicker.

I did not expect it to be easy. I focused on the ending and on how I would feel once I made my way through this hardship. When you think about it, each individual is the only person who can control how he or she feels, and although you may say that others will have an influence on your feelings, that influence only happens if YOU allow it.

The Mind is the Key

Your mind is the remote control to everything. If you want others to influence how you will feel, then you can make that happen. However, you can choose to filter what is happening around you and decide to manage events differently than others. Life events will always happen, and how you choose to manage them will either move you forward in life or keep you in the "loop."

Unexpected events do not come with a warning or signal to give you a "heads up" that they are coming. They appear just like large icebergs in the water. Although there are things you can do to best prepare for an event, this still does not necessarily stop the event from happening.

Think through your life right now. Is there an event that comes to mind where you took action to prevent something from occurring? You may have had success in preventing it, or maybe no matter what you did you were not able to prevent the event from occurring.

An unexpected event can be hard, extremely hard, and can shake you out of your current reality for a while. However, remember that it is your mindset that will direct your actions and be the key to how you will respond. You do have a choice on how best to maneuver through it.

The Second Unplanned Event

During the creation of this book, I encountered another unexpected event. I had been writing for months and had ten chapters written when the unthinkable happened, something I never expected.

My computer crashed. A virus had killed the operating system along with my hard drive. Throughout the process of writing the chapters, I was periodically backing up the book to an external hard drive but had not done a recent backup. When my computer crashed I did not realize how severe the issue was, especially since it had crashed in the past and all the files had been recovered.

I took my computer to the Geek Squad. The first team called back after a few days and informed me they could not get to the files. They said, "We have a SUPER Geek Squad team located in Kentucky and your computer would be shipped to them to begin the recovery."

After they informed me of this, I was feeling confident that this would be resolved. I thought that since this is where all the hard tech things go, of course these men and women are the best at what they do. Surely they would be able to get the information from my hard drive. They did inform me it would take two to three months before I would have a response.

I was shocked! Two to three months! I was upset, although I still felt good since I truly believed they could get the files. I did not stop writing and I continued on with my next chapter, this time backing up daily.

The Call

Finally, a call came. It was "the call," you know—the one you want with the "good" news!

"Mr. Hall, your computer is ready for pickup!"

I felt overjoyed yet confused because the caller did not say anything about my hard drive. I called back and quickly asked, "They mentioned my computer was ready for pickup and I was wondering if all the files were restored?"

"Can I have your name, sir?"

I responded, "Last name HALL, first name Cardiff."

Silence on the other end. Then, *"We were not able to recover any files."*

I repeated what I heard. "No files?"

"Yes, no files."

It happened. Everything I created was GONE, taken away from me.

The unexpected had happened. Reality sunk in. So I thought, "How I can create the same content again that would be the same as before?" And something mentally kicked in and I heard a voice say, "YOU CAN."

Just a few days after this, I spoke to my friend Chris to let him know what had happened regarding my hard drive crashing, and he said, *"If you need to rewrite it, it will be better because you have grown."*

Relinquish the W/S/C of Focus

That statement hit me hard. But it also helped me keep my focus away from the "would've, should've, could've, mentality."

I made a decision to begin rewriting immediately. Could I recall every single paragraph and detail that I had written previously? No, but I did start again with clarity and a fervor to communicate the best to you in the new version of my book.

That is what I knew must be done. I did not have a pity party for myself. I just dug in and began to work. I did not look at what occurred as time wasted. It fact, it had molded me into the person I am today.

When the unexpected event does happen, you have a choice. I had a choice to stop writing and never finish the book, or feel sorry for myself and blame whoever created the computer virus, or simply to start again.

Vision Provides Clarity

I have discussed having a vision. My vision is why I started over to write a book. I did not truly have a choice because my vision is driving me, just as your vision can drive you through unexpected events as well. Having a vision and holding on to that vision can help push you through any unexpected events.

The next way to push through an unexpected event is your attitude. Your attitude will determine what you can accomplish. Stop and ask yourself, "How do I feel when I have a bad attitude? Do I feel like doing something extra? Do I feel overwhelmed and frustrated?"

When you have a bad attitude, your body language is not good and does not exert good energy. You may behave irrationally and make poor decisions.

Have a Positive Attitude, No Matter What Happens

Having a positive attitude gives you more energy as well as the ability to think through what is happening. Now, I am not saying having a positive attitude will make the event go away, but it will give you the power to better handle the uncertainties.

You have the power to control your attitude. You can allow the event to force what your attitude should be, or you can decide to take a deep breath and mentally create the right attitude when the unexpected arises.

Surround Yourself with Positive People

The last way to help you through your unexpected event is to surround yourself with positive individuals who will provide support. Having someone or a group of people to support you is powerful, especially if they have gone through the same or similar situations.

The weight of the unexpected event will not be heavy because the individual or group is absorbing the weight. This can help you feel better. When you are connected to someone or a group who has journeyed through that event, you have the ability to ask questions and gain feedback, which is powerful and can help you move through the event much faster.

When I lost the chapters, my coach at the time provided me with the support and belief that helped me move past the tragedy. Just having him believe in me was the fuel I needed to power my efforts.

Get a Confidante

If you do not have a coach or someone in whom you can confide, seek someone out. Perhaps it could be a good friend who is a good listener and does not judge you, or it could be someone you know or a group that offers support. Whoever it is, connect with them and be willing to accept their support.

Unexpected events will happen to you in your life's journey and how you handle such an event, will show much about your character and tenacity. No one is immune to unexpected events.

Les Brown, motivational speaker and author sums up the unexpected event like this, *"Anytime you suffer a setback or disappointment, put your head down and plow ahead."*

Key Points

- The unexpected event will happen during your life journey. However, you have a choice in how you will respond.
- Remove these words from your mind: would've, should've, and could've. They are not serving you and they limit your potential.
- Your vision is your lighthouse that leads you to your destination.
- The rudder that can steer you through the unexpected event is your attitude.
- Having the support of others will provide comfort and strength.
- Don't be tethered to the "Why Me buoy." Instead, take action.
- Inside your mind is where you will either allow the unexpected event to hold you down or you will use it to propel you forward.

Chapter 4
The Wave of Failure

Experiences Can Lead to the Path of Achievement

Failure; just the word can send signals to your brain. You may be feeling something right now just by reading the word FAILURE. What is that for you? Perhaps it is a sense of sadness, regret, or emptiness. This word has such deep meaning and the origin of it is rooted deeply in us.

Remember back to grade school, when you were first able to understand what grades meant? A, B, C, D, and well they skipped E and went to F. When grades came out, I remember asking my friends, "Hey, what did you get on the test?"

It seemed everyone in the circle was waiting to hear about the person who got an F. The F indicated you failed the test and did not pass. From such a young age we are taught that failure is bad, time after time, even in college. When you received an F it meant that you did not do enough to get a passing grade. If you failed too many classes, you were asked to leave school.

Failure Has Deep Roots

When you think about it, for eighteen or more years of school, you were ingrained with the belief that it is bad to receive an F, that if you have this grade, you are labeled a failure. For most people the word failure has been deeply rooted in their soul since they were young, and has hindered many people today from trying something because they did not want to be reminded of the past.

The ingrained years of failure have conditioned many to not enter the realm of possibilities; instead, they stay locked within the gates of imprisonment.

I'm here to tell you, you are bigger than your past! Allow your failure not to define you but to mold you.

Have you ever pulled one of those weeds with a deep root in a flower garden? If so, you know it takes time to dig it out. And you know you need the right equipment to help pull out that weed. The same is true with the weed called FAILURE. But the good news is, there are several things you can do to help remove that deeply rooted weed so you can begin to grow.

Seek to Fail with a Shift in Mindset

The first way to help remove that deeply rooted weed is to FAIL. I know you are saying, really? Yes, you must seek to fail and alter your mindset around failure. Believe it or not, to fail is actually GOOD.

Winston Churchill summed up success this way. *"Success is the ability to go from one failure to another with no loss of enthusiasm."*

He mentioned that success comes from shifting how you think about failure. This may sound twisted, but if you look at failure as good, then failure would not stop you, would it?

Richard Fenton and Andrea Waltz wrote a great book titled *GO for NO!* You may be asking, "Do I really need to 'GO for NO!'?" The answer is YES. Seeking to "GO for NO!" is seeking to fail. When you read the book you will realize what lies ahead in your journey, if you have the mindset that failing is something good not bad.

Learn from Failure

Seeing failure as something positive is a complete shift from what most people have been taught about failing, since failure has not been looked at as something positive.

To achieve success, one must be willing to fail and fail again. When you fail, learn something from that failure. By doing this it can help loosen your deeply rooted belief that failure is bad. When you fail, take the time to look at exactly what factors contributed to why you came up short.

Failing Leads to Results

Failure is seen time and time again in various sports. In baseball, a batter has the chance to swing at pitches to hit the ball. When the batter does not hit the ball and three strikes are called by the umpire, an out is created and the batter strikes out.

If you look at the statistics for the number of times at bat and hits, a good hitter makes contact with the ball only 30% percent of the time. This is called the batting average. When you think about it, seven out of 10 times the batter FAILS.

One of the greatest baseball players was George Herman, also known as, Babe Ruth, who struck out 1,330 times and had a batting average of 34.2% with 2,873 hits in his major league career.[1] He said, *"Every strike brings me closer to the next home run."*

The batter's mindset upon getting up to the plate to bat is not one of "I want to strike out." It is "I want to make a hit now." The coach could instruct the hitter to take a walk (meaning to get on base without trying to hit the ball). A batter is always making the effort to get better, to improve their batting average.

Analyze Failure

When you fail, you should look at what you could do better. Take some notes on what you did well and also the things upon which you could improve. Batters do this. They analyze their swing, work on their position, take batting practice, and study pitchers so they understand their tendencies, in order to improve their batting average and help their team win. Think about what you can do to improve from your failure and simply decide to do it.

Seek to have help, which can loosen the roots of failure.

Do you remember a game in grade school called tug of war, where you and other kids pull on a rope to bring the flag across to your side?

Everyone in the team pulling together caused the flag to cross on your side. The same can occur in your life, if you allow someone or a group of individuals to help loosen the grip of failure. Take time to analyze failure in the bonus materials found at www.cardiffdhall.com/resources.

Get A Coach, Get A Game Plan

There are personal coaches available to help individuals achieve. These coaches provide the necessary game plan to help you turn failure into success. Going back to the batting example where the batter is working on attempting to increase his or her batting average, there is a coach helping, guiding, and giving tips.

A personal coach can do the same, and you need to believe someone can help you. I have a personal coach, and it has been life-changing to have someone guide me, believing I can do more. This coach pushes me and has helped loosen the grips of failure and propelled me forward in life.

Find that someone or group of individuals who can help you loosen any roots of failure you encounter, so you can grow and achieve.

View Failure Successfully Short

Webster has a short and to the point definition of failure. It is simply "the lack of success."

Did you notice the word *success*? The definition isn't focusing on the failure, it merely states the lack, meaning not having enough. Make your mind understand you didn't fail; you were just successfully short of failure. The famous Thomas Edison quote can be adapted this way.

> *"I have not failed, I have successfully found 10,000 ways that will not work."*

Edison took his failure and looked at it simply as a number. He failed over 10,000 times, and yet did not quit. You must have the fortitude and mindset like Thomas Edison and look at failure as the road to achievement.

Quitting Robs You of Your Future

Quitting is not part of the process along the road to achievement and is always the easiest way out. Failure is part of the process and knowing this can help you remain upright, just like the buoy which remains upright despite the waves that hit it. When you quit, it has an impact on you and on others around you.

People are always watching you, whether they actually let you know it or not. The course to achievement includes failure. Along the way you may have a strong desire to quit, especially after repeated effort to produce the results you want. You have a choice to keep going or to give up. But follow Thomas Edison's footsteps and do not give up.

"Our greatest glory is not in never failing,
but in rising every time we fail."

Confucius

Key Points

- Failures are ingrained at an early age and have deep roots into adulthood.
- Utilize your failures to grow, so you can be untethered from the past.
- Increasing the times you fail can propel you forward, if you are learning from your failures.
- What one may classify as failure can be seen by another person as success.
- Take time to review the actions that led you to successfully fall short, in order to increase your ability to advance.
- Find someone who can provide guidance.
- Do not allow your failures to define who you are. Instead, let them define how resilient you are.

CHAPTER 5
THE WAVE OF CHOICES

YOUR GPS

D o you like making choices? I love choices. They give you the opportunity to decide what you feel is important to you for your vision.

Choices Defined

Imagine a body of water. You've been asked to build a dock, even though you are not skilled in wood-making. There are many choices you need to consider, to build the dock. Here are just a few. What type of wood would you use? How wide would the floorboards be? What is the length of the dock? How will the dock be anchored? What tools will be needed? All of these questions are necessary for the creation of the dock. They require decisions since there are multiple possibilities. Making choices are part of the process of making a decision when faced with varying options.

Would you begin building the dock without having made all of the choices above? I trust you said no. There is preplanning, making decisions on the questions and mapping out your plan to complete the dock. What if you just started building with no plan at all, using the "I'm-just-going-to-wing-it design"? Which, by the way, doesn't come with any guarantee. Maybe you've been reacting to life with that type of attitude instead of purpose vision-based living. The wonderful beauty of life is that you are the owner of your decisions. Allow this truth to seep into your mind.

The power to make decisions rests in your hands through the choices you make. You have the power to decide how you feel, what type of clothes you wear, what you eat, what way you will drive to reach your destination…and the list goes on and on. Making choices is taking personal responsibility, whether small or big, that will affect you along your journey.

The great Eleanor Roosevelt said this about taking personal responsibility for choices. *"In the long run, we shape our lives, and we shape ourselves. The process never ends until we die. And the choices we make are ultimately our own responsibility."*

You have the power to decide, which starts in your mind. As your mind processes information, you tell it to make decisions based on your visions for your life.

The ability for the mind to actively process something and make a decision about a choice can happen in less than a second. You do not even realize your mind actively doing this, even when you simply make a choice about what clothes to wear today.

Although the overall decision-making process may have taken a long time about what clothes to wear today, your mind actually went through the sorting very quickly and a choice was made. You probably did not feel the gears in your head turning; it was you who controlled the process and the output.

Your Choices Define Who You Are—Whether You Like It or Not

Choices define you. Whether you consider them big or small, they still have an impact on who you are and who you become. Choices can teach lessons, if you desire to learn from them. I have personally made many choices that have taught me valuable lessons.

Prior to having a vision for my life, I made choices that impacted me financially. Without a vision, I was drawn to all of the pictures you've seen—cool clothes, beautiful vacations, and more. I had the philosophy of thinking that "if you want something, just pay for it on credit." Credit was money to me. The mantra—have now and pay later—just fit with the philosophy I was living without a vision.

There were credit cards available with zero interest financing, and companies were bombarding this message in ads. And I was drawn in by the advertising and made the choice to live a life on credit, which was great at the time since it allowed me to have nice things I could not afford otherwise.

I remember working out of my home office one afternoon and my wife was working during the day at her job. In town, there was a travel agency, and I had this idea to go to Hawaii! Yes, we needed a vacation to Hawaii. I recall seeing an ad on TV, and guess what, the ad worked. I drove to the agency, met with an awesome lady, and we booked a vacation at the main island and Maui using... any guesses? Yes, credit. Just like that, a swipe of the card and you have a vacation. Airfare for two plus, 4-star hotels and rental cars. Did I wonder how I was going to eventually pay for this trip? Not really, given at the time there was no anchor to any vision.

Slowly over time, my financial choices led me to a deep hole, and eventually, into unpaid taxes and a lien placed against my house.

The financial choices I made over time accumulated to put me in a position of paying high interest rates and owing money to many creditors. This created a sunken feeling in my stomach. All of these issues led to bad credit, which impacted what type of loans I received for a mortgage as well as interest rates on auto loans and much more.

All of the financial choices I made had snowballed and created an unpleasant outcome in my life. Once you are in a place like this, you can either run away from it or face it head on and begin to repair it. What took a few years to destroy took too many years to rebuild.

I was connected to a financial expert who showed me how to repair the damage done, and slowly over time, piece by piece, I paid off all the loans and creditors, and my credit was restored.

Perhaps my financial choices resonate with you, and if so, hopefully you can learn from them like I did. A poor financial choice made one time will probably not affect you; however, if continued time after time, these choices will have a major impact in your life. The average U.S. household is carrying $15,779 in credit card debt.[1]

So where are you regarding the U.S. household debt in your household?

What would better life choices mean to you? Learning from our choices can give us valuable life lessons and help us create a better life, even though these lessons can sometimes be very painful. Personally, I am grateful for having gone through this experience and having learned now how to make smarter financial decisions.

Today is a Result of Past Choices

Where are you in your life now, as a result of the choices you have made? All of your choices have led you to where you are today. That may seem hard to grasp, but it is true. There are a few things you can do that will help you make better decisions. The first is to accept personal responsibility for your life now.

Where you are in your job, your financial position, where you live, the impact you have made in your community, the friends you have the relationships you have… these are just a few of the situations that are a result of choices you have made.

Select The Right Mindset

You could argue that some of what has occurred in your life is a result of the choices of others and that you did not have any input. Although that may be true to some extent, that mindset does not embrace taking full personal accountability for your life. Remember, it is not the set of circumstances in which you are born that counts but how you choose to react to those circumstances. You have the freedom to choose your mental attitude and to make decisions to change the outcome.

Personal Reasonability with No Excuses

The word responsible is defined by Merriam-Webster as "the state of being the person who caused something to happen." Being responsible, you cause something to happen, positive or negative. However, do not associate negativity with that statement; instead, focus on causing something positive, and see mistakes as learning experiences and not as something negative.

All you have accomplished and have yet to accomplish depends upon the personal choices you make.

"You must take personal responsibility.
You cannot change the circumstances, the seasons,
or the wind, but you can change yourself."

Jim Rhone

The word personal means ownership, and the sole stockholder in your life is you! Others may influence you but you truly have the final decision.

When you are willing to take personal or sole owner-ship for being responsible by the creation of the vision for your life, you realize you can make choices that will allow movement toward that vision. You remove any resentment and begin to take control of your choices.

Imagine if everyone around you accepted responsibility of their choices and took control of their life. Not allowing blame, resentment, and bitterness to be attached to the choices they made or not having the life they desired.

Ownership Your Future Will Say Thank You

Although you cannot control what others do, you are the only one who can personally make the decision to control your own life. It can start with you and if you have not yet accepted personal responsibility, why not? Doing it today will make all the difference in your future.

The word ownership is the right to possess something. By taking ownership, you get to decide, you get to take control. It all begins and ends with your choices, which will impact your future. Inside the Tide Turner resources, you can make a commitment to take ownership of your choices found at www.cardiffdhall.com/resources.

Congrats for making the decision to have full owner-ship of your choices! Accept personal responsibility and know you are the one who is in control of your choices. Everything you have done and yet to do are a result of these choices. Embrace your ownership and you can achieve anything.

Priorities–It Begins Here

You must decide what is important to you. Then clearly define the choices you need to make so they're a part of your vision. Deciding what is important allows you to make better decisions, which should be aligned with your vision. What would you say if I were to ask you, "What is important to you?" Think about this, take the time. What is it for you?

- Family
- Job
- Volunteering
- Money
- Faith
- Purpose or Mission
- Hobby

Depending on the priorities in your life, you might mention one, several, or all of these. It will be important to revisit these throughout your life. As you grow into a new version of you, your priorities will change, so be prepared. Your vision will remain firm while your priorities might be adjusted.

Vision + Priorities = Choices

Your vision and what is important to you must drive your choices. If family is important, the choices you make should be connected to your family. Let us imagine family is the most important thing in your life and your employer has offered you a great job in Europe for a year and they are requiring you to relocate. The job will also require you to travel extensively, which will significantly reduce the time you spend with your family.

You need to ask two questions. Is this potential overseas job aligned to my vision? Is this job aligned to what is important to me at this moment in my life? Understanding the responses to these questions will enable you to make a sound decision and the responses will be congruent to your vision.

When your choices are not congruent, you generate a magnetic pull that will cause undue stress and imbalance in your life.

Do You Want Aliveness and Joy?

Deciding on what is most important to you is also a choice. You must understand what gives you enjoyment and what makes you feel alive. This is the substance that will deliver purpose in your life. These are the things that can ultimately help you make your decisions about what is important to you.

Aliveness comes from understanding your choices, and once you do that, you have more energy, you are able to see things clearly and you have a new spirit within you. When you have aliveness and joy, your confidence is higher and your outlook on your life improves.

Sticking to Your Commitments

What commitments would you like to accomplish? Think about them. Why haven't you accomplished them yet? Perhaps it is taking longer than expected. Perhaps you started and just gave up. Perhaps you haven't even started and you are in delay mode. No matter the reason, all of the choices you've made regarding your commitments have taken you to where you are now.

When I started writing this book, I made the intentional choice to work on it for a minimum of 15 minutes per day. I elevated this choice to ensure I made it a top priority. In a Darren Daily post by Darren Hardy, he talked about his book, *The Compound Effect*.

"The Compound Effect is the principle of reaping huge rewards from a series of small, smart choices." [2]

What small smart choices can you make today? Here are a few ideas that can help you increase your commitment level.

Intentional Action Over a Period of Time

Many of you might be thinking it is not possible to complete a book just by writing 15 minutes per day. But you are now reading the finished book because of a choice I made, and a choice I continued to make every single day until this manuscript was completed. Keep in mind that a continuous action over a period of time will eventually lead to completion. This is one of the keys to lasting success. Every day you will have a choice to make on whether to keep the commitment to yourself or not.

Evaluate The Long Term Impact of Your Choices

Before you make a choice you need to ensure you are aware of the impact that choice will have, not only immediately but also in the long term. Having such an awareness of the impact can help you make better choices. When I mentioned the impact of your choices, I am referencing the choices you make daily and once compounded over time, which Darren Hardy discusses makes an imprint on your life.

A good question to ask yourself is this: *Is what I am about to do going to help me in the future?* If your future could talk with you, would it be aligned with your decision?

If I asked you what an impactful choice meant to you, what would you say? Impactful choices are those that have the strongest effect on your life. These need to be carefully examined so that you are making the best decision. Allocate more of your energy toward significant choices that will have a positive impact on your life.

Vital to Receive Advice

When making a choice that has impact, it is advisable to discuss it with someone such as a trusted friend, spouse, or coach. Receiving input will allow you to see much more than your own perspective. It is said that when looking for something, a second pair of eyes is better than just your own set of eyes, and the same holds true when making a big choice that will impact you and those around you. It is good to have someone who will challenge your choice and help you look at it differently.

Don't Lose Sight of the Big Vision for Your Life

Neither you nor I can predict the future, but when deciding on something, you should visualize how the choice you make could benefit you. When thinking about how this choice will impact you long term, take time to write down how you believe the choice is aligned with your vision. Realizing the impact of the decision will allow you to make better decisions and allow those big decisions to fit within your vision.

You make choices every day, and the daily choices you make can be simple and not require much thought, just action. There are other choices that come along during your journey that have more substance and require time.

If you accept personal responsibility for your choices, realize what is important to you and understand the impact of the choices you are making. If you do this, you will make better choices in your life and you will look at making choices with positivity rather than as a chore.

Choices give you freedom to decide, and ultimately, it is you who must decide.

Nelson Mandela said this about choices,

"May your choices reflect your hopes, not your fears."

Choices define who you are and who you will become, and represent the hopes you have. Choose today to make better choices, to give yourself the benefit of knowing you have taken ownership of all choices in your life.

Key Points

- Choices offer options and the ability to take ownership.
- Where you are right now in life is a result of the choices made.
- A poor choice made one time will not impact your life while poor choices consistently made will compound and have a negative impact.
- Allow your choices to be aligned with your vision and priorities.
- Thinking long term and understanding how your choices will impact the future will generate better choices.
- Look to gain advice from others to help direct your choices.
- Choices are the pathway, which will lead you forward or push you back. Your choices will define you.

CHAPTER 6
THE WAVE OF HABITS
YOU ARE THE ARTIST

The artist designs and creates; you do the same with your habits.

Habits are a routine of behavior that you do consistently over time. Through ongoing repetition, certain behaviors become automatic and unconscious. Habits can be helpful or harmful. When you woke up this morning, you had several habits in which you engaged. You may not think of them as habits; instead, you may think of them as routines.

Habits can form into a routine. Along the journey of life, you will pick up habits that can help you achieve success—since success leaves clues and habits are one of the clues. When you think about your morning habits, do you realize how you may have developed those habits in the first place? Perhaps you were raised to do certain things in the morning when you were young and you continue to do them now.

Habits can be learned from others, from our parents, from someone we trust; in fact, from anyone who influences us, including television and social media, if you allow that for yourself.

What Creates a Habit?

A habit is a repeated action over time. Doing something once does not create a habit. For example, let us say you make the decision today to get your workout completed in the morning and you do it. Only you find out that you did not enjoy the workout in the morning so you decide not to do it again.

Repetition creates the habit, and being willing to use discipline and intention can help in shaping the habit. Habits take time to form.

Dr. Maxwell Maltz wrote a book in the 1960s where he said that it takes twenty-one days to form a habit. Dr. Maltz mentioned that it would take that long for an old mental image of yourself to dissolve and a new one to gel. The thought of twenty-one days, established by Dr. Maltz and written 56 years ago, seems to become fact today, yet there are behaviors where it will take the brain longer to learn the new behavior and thus gel into a habit.[1]

The amount of time a habit takes to form is dependent upon you. Meanwhile, at the core you have to begin to shape the habit. If you do something daily, the habit will form within twenty-one days, but if done every other week, the action will take longer to become a habit.

You have the power to choose the amount of time you spend on a particular action and know you hold the keys to the habits you create for yourself.

Your Environment Influences You

Perhaps you have heard this statement, "You are a product of your environment." You may choose or not choose to believe this, but habits are influenced by your environment and by those with whom you spend your time. This includes watching your favorite programs, listening to your favorite singers, or reading your favorite authors.

Think about your childhood and the environment in which you lived. This may bring back great memories or it may bring back chilling memories. If it was a positive environment, you probably picked up a habit from watching or experiencing someone else performing the said habit. Of course, you could have also picked up negative habits.

I can remember my mom being the planner, always writing lists and giving us lists to complete. When I think about myself, I realize my habit of making lists was modeled by my mother. Who has influenced you in the development of a habit? Maybe it is a family member, co-worker, friend, a mentor, a pastor, your spouse, a coach, or someone with whom you have interacted on a frequent basis. Or it could be someone you have met only once or even just read about.

There are many individuals in your life today that may influence your habits. If you surround yourself with the right people, over time you will mirror them and your habits will be eventually formed. If you see someone who has achieved what you are aiming for, you will want to spend time with them and do what they do. The environment or people you spend your time with will begin to shape your habits.

Pay Attention to Your Habits

Habits can either harm you or help you in the achievement of your goals. Along your journey in life you may develop poor habits that impede your progress to achieve. You need to look at good habits as the tools needed to assist you in helping navigate your waters. Bad habits do not supply the tools you need. Instead, they remove the tools needed and thus rob you of the opportunity to move forward in the journey.

Depending upon the vision you have for your life, you can identify what habits will help and what habits will harm you. Look at your life right now and figure out if there are any bad habits you need to eliminate. Are there any that are constricting your potential? If so, decide to remove them now. Get around people who can help you. It can be a group, a coach, or someone who can help you break and eliminate the habit before it does more harm to you and those around you.

Cultivate Good Habits through Daily Effort

Good habits give you the ability to grow. One of the habits I created for myself was to invest in knowledge and information by reading books. Not the kind of books where the author takes you on a fictional story or adventure, but books that provide content that help shape you, develop your character, and increase practical knowledge that can help you achieve your goals.

Reading the right books, like this one, is an example of putting the right tool in the toolbox that will help you along your journey. Develop good habits that will enable and allow you to reach your potential.

Goods habits must be a part of your daily routine.

> *"You'll never change your life until you change something daily. The secret of your success is found in your daily routine."*

John Maxwell

Decide You Are Responsible

I mentioned bad habits could harm you and impede your journey in your waters. And only you have the power to eliminate bad habits from your life. There are a number of ways to do that and it all starts with YOU. You need to ensure your habits are aligned with your vision. "Is this habit aligned with who I want to become?" is a powerful question to answer. If you allow yourself to answer truthfully, you are practicing self-actualization, which is the ability to become fully aware of yourself.

If you know you have a bad habit impacting what you want to accomplish, you have a choice. You can continue to engage in that habit and not achieve what you want, or you can make the decision to work on eradicating that habit.

First and foremost, you must accept personal responsibility for the creation of the habit. You can blame others, but at its core, you created that habit.

Bad Habits Have Depth

Think of the bad habit like an old rusted anchor that is several miles down into the ocean off of your boat. You simply cannot pull it up by yourself. You will need others to help you get the right equipment and pull the anchor out of you. Is it painful? Yes, it can be. Is going through some pain worth it to remove the anchor, so you can move forward in your journey?

Bad Habits, If Not Attended, Can Turn into Addiction

I have a great friend who developed an addiction that was destroying his work and family life. He made the commitment to put himself in treatment, which required him to be removed from his family and friends and closed off from the world he knew. I sent him notes and information via the mail to lift his spirits, and to tell him I was proud that he was taking responsibility.

Today, he is a much better husband, father, and friend. Once the anchor was removed, he continued to seek support to ensure it did not come back. If you have this philosophy, "I don't really have a problem anymore and I can handle it myself," your anchor will come back. Make sure you stay around those who can help you from falling back into old habitual ways.

Eliminating bad habits can take time and energy. If you have a bad habit today and you want to achieve, make a decision right now and write this down.

"Today I decide to eliminate my bad habit of _____ and I will seek the necessary help to remove the anchor that I have created, because I have goals and dreams I want to accomplish along my journey."

Date:

Signature:

Allow yourself to be free of your bad habits so you can receive the fullness of your life. Write additional notes in your free resource at www.cardiffdhall.com/resources.

Good Habits Start in the Mind

Good habits are developed, and there are a few ways to create those habits that will help you along your journey. Creating a good habit first starts in your mind. Your mind controls the actions, and thus, your mind must be positioned correctly to help you stay on track and toward creating a good habit.

Your self-talk, that which you tell yourself, must be aligned to the habit you are developing. For example, imagine you are trying to develop a habit of not eating fast food, but then you tell yourself, "I love double cheeseburgers and just one double cheeseburger is not going to hurt me."

Your subconscious mind then accepts what you have told yourself, and therefore, since it agrees with the statement, you stop by your favorite fast food place and eat that double cheeseburger. Your new habit is broken. Just that one simple thought to yourself can sabotage your efforts to create a new habit. Controlling what you say to yourself will influence the development of a new habit, either positively or negatively.

Accountability Partners Can Help

Another way you can develop a good habit is to find an accountability partner, someone who will keep you accountable and who believes in you. That person is someone you should talk to on a frequent basis about your goals and your feelings. A good accountability partner should be someone who listens well, someone who has your best interests at heart, and someone you can trust.

Do not feel that your accountability partner needs to be developing the same habit. The individual needs to have the ability to ask questions and challenge you.

With the progress of removing the bad habit, it is important to replace that bad habit with a good habit. What you do not want to occur is to remove the anchor and develop another anchor that does not free you to move forward. Your accountability partner will help you ensure something positive comes in place of the habit you are removing.

Reinforce Good Habits

Your accountability partner will help you strengthen your discipline toward developing the good habit. Habits only happen once the action is repeated on a regular basis, so you must make sure you take the necessary steps to reinforce the new habit.

You should block out time in your schedule, allocating it to develop your new habit. If you do not make it a priority in your schedule for the day, you will allow something to get in the way and the action will not occur.

When scheduling time, know how much you will allocate to your daily action. Finally, you must do the work and take the action needed on a daily basis, so your positive action becomes a habit. Seek the right habits to help you move along your journey, so the anchor does not keep you in one place and prevent you from moving toward your vision.

"We become what we repeatedly do."

Sean Covey

Key Points

- Habits are born with intention and consistent repeated action over a period of time.
- Your choices have created the habits you currently have today.
- The influences in your life and environment you place yourself in will shape your habits
- Daily habits are often overlooked; given that they have been anchored for years.
- Development of new habits start within the mind and when you decide to remove your anchor.
- A poor habit which has been anchored for years will require the actions of accountability partners.
- Allow your habits to push you forward in your journey.

CHAPTER 7
THE WAVE OF PORTS
THE COURSE YOU DRIVE ON

Ports are places you decide to anchor and reside in life. Each port creates who you are. It has its own characteristics, and you may find yourself in any one of these ports with your anchor down until you decide to pull it up.

The five ports you have the ability to anchor are:

1. Learning
2. Me, Myself, and I
3. Comfort
4. Growth
5. Contribution

If you had to guess what port you are at today, what would you say? This may be hard to answer at this time; meanwhile, by the end of this wave, you will be able to understand what port you are anchored to.

The **Learning Port** is the only port truly defined by age. The other ports are not defined by age, and you are the only one who can decide if you stay, move, or advance through any of the remaining ports.

True success and fulfillment is achieved when you advance to the final ports of **Growth and Contribution**. I encourage you to aspire to the final ports so you are fully making your contribution to the world. Do not allow yourself to think contribution should be left up to someone else. Those who reach their potential in the final port have a mindset of "What is Possible" and look to contribute. Allow yourself to have this mindset so you can make an impact on others.

PORT 1: The Learning Port

The first port we all go through is **Learning**. This port begins when you are an infant. During this port you learn how to cry for food and how to crawl. You learn how to stand up by yourself with the help of furniture as you steady your legs. You stand up, and then you fall down. And you continue to repeat the process until eventually, you take your first steps.

As you grow during this port, you continue to learn how to do things on your own. Your help comes from parents, from teachers, and from those around you. They help you learn so you can be a functioning person.

The Goal of Port 1

The goal of the learning phase is to build knowledge and practical guidance for living in the world. In this port you do not have a choice of learning. You have to attend school, for example, and learn information that you believe may or may not help you in life.

One of the best classes I ever took that gave me a very important practical skill for living in today's world was typing. I am very grateful for that typewriting class, which was taught using a Brothers typewriter. These typewriters are antiques now and if you have not seen a typewriter, Google it. This class was offered in high school, and at the time, I was not impressed with learning how to correctly type, but this was not a choice. It was a requirement, so I learned how to do it. This one skill that I learned many years ago has stayed with me and I continue to use it.

Learning in this port can develop skills that can benefit you for life. Learning continues in post high school graduation courses in technical schools and in universities, where you learn skills that are targeted to your desired field.

In this port, you learn to take care of yourself with the help of parents, grandparents, and leaders in organizations, i.e., those who care about preparing you for life on your own.

The learning port is vast since so much knowledge comes to you from birth to your mid 20s. It does not matter if you did or did not want to go through this stage; this is not a voluntary port. Learning is part of the process of life in this important port of education.

"Education is what remains after one has forgotten what one has learned in school."

Albert Einstein

PORT 2: Me, Myself, and I

The anchor is lifted and you head to the **Me, Myself, and I** port. This port is where all of the attention is focused on you. You are focused on yourself. Everything you do is centered on you. Typically, this phase comes after graduation from high school or college; however, this is a port where many people keep their anchor in. One way to understand if you are in this port is you have the mindset that it is not your responsibility to help anyone.

During this port, there is a sense of "What is mine is mine, and I earned it." At this port, individuals are highly concerned about their appearance, which is focused on the exterior, instead of the interior makeup of their heart. This port is often seen in sports, where an individual feels they are more important than the team itself.

The "ME" Focused Football Player

One example that comes to mind is a player who played on the Dallas Cowboys football team. His actions on and off the field were driven by the mentality of "Hey world, look at ME!" He would throw tantrums on the sideline, yell at his coaches, and say things against his team.

When he was in the spotlight, his actions outside of football were the same, and everything was focused on him. Eventually, the team cut him and he is not in football anymore. His "me" focus pushed him out of the football world. When people are in this stage, there is not any deep care for those around them. Individuals in this stage have a deep desire to be noticed and will never do things they believe serve others more than themselves. One can transition through this port if one chooses, but some remain stuck.

To move forward, to become your greatest self, you must not linger in this port. You must wind up the anchor and decide to leave this port.

PORT 3: Comfort

Comfort is the Captain's seat of mediocrity. Imagine being in your favorite chair, couch, or the place in your home where it feels great to nap, relax, or just sit. Comfort is defined as the state of ease, and this is the stage many aspire to reach, where life is not so stressful and there is a sense of calmness.

This stage can take many years to reach. And once you reach it, you may not wish to stretch for your goals or dreams, but rather, you would like to sit in the captain's seat of mediocrity. To be comfortable is not about stretching, reaching beyond your comfort zone, or facing your fears. It is about remaining in the status quo with the lack of motivation.

"People who are unable to motivate themselves must be content with mediocrity, no matter how impressive their other talents."

Andrew Carnegie

The Captain's seat may feel great; however, if you want to achieve and reach your potential, clinging to the seat is not the way to get there.

The Fear of Leaving the Chair

Not everyone is hardwired to break out of the comfort port. Going beyond just being comfortable is a decision one has to make. Imagine sitting on a tropical island. The air temperature is just right. It is not too hot. The palm trees are swaying to a light breeze and the ocean is calm. You sit in your beach chair reading a book and you are comfortable. Life at this moment is great. Since you are comfortable, leaving this tropical paradise is not a possibility you want to consider.

Leaving the Captain's seat causes fear of the unknown. In the comfort port, you are not focused on pushing yourself or learning new things, because this requires effort and being comfortable is not about exerting yourself. The comfort port is where dreams are lost and the imagination is at a standstill. While in this stage, those who have dreams look at their circumstances and choose not to take the action necessary to live out their dreams. Individuals allow the peacefulness and the comfort of the chair to take over their ability to try to push themselves outside of their comfort zone.

Pushing, creating new habits, and failing are not in the mind of one who resides in this port. Why break away from the warmth of comfort just to get cold? Many individuals enjoy this port given the port provides a place for avoidance.

"Life begins at the end of your comfort zone."

Neale Donald Walsch

Comfort Can Rob You of Pursuing Your Dreams

Comfort can be the silent destroyer of your dreams. If you are willing to leave the comfort port and are willing to be uncomfortable, you can have the opportunity to experience the visions you hold inside your mind. The door is always open for you to move away from the Captain's seat of mediocrity.

Erica McCuen, Tide Turner, Author Academy Elite member, and author of *You Taught My Feet to Dance* walked through the door and took the leap of faith by moving away from comfort. Erica went through sorrow and suffering, and felt compelled from God that her story could help others despite not having the financial resources to commit to a program such as Author Academy Elite.

She decided to step out of her fear and listened to what her creator God was asking her to do, which was to share her sorrow, pain, suffering, and healing to help others who find themselves in the pit she was in and climbed out of. Although those closest to her didn't agree that she should step out in faith and become financially strapped, she was pulled more by God's grace. Below is her story in her own words.

My greatest dream in life was to be a wife and mother. I love family and I longed to be married for life so I could pass that legacy down to my children as my parents and grandparents did for me. My dream was fulfilled when I became a pastor's wife and mommy.

For 15 years we had the honor to minister to thousands. We were also miraculously blessed with five beautiful children whom I was privileged to stay at home with. However, behind closed doors, things were extremely dysfunctional.

Tragically, in June of 2009, my dream died. I became a single mother to my children ages 12, 9, 6, 3 and 10 months old. Within a few months after that, my husband completely abandoned us. I was left not only to raise our children in the midst of my severe grief, but I was also forced to try and find some way to make income in order to provide for them.

Thankfully, my wonderful, godly parents took us in for two years. They were instrumental in helping us heal. My dad graciously became a fill-in-father and selflessly provided for us on his retirement budget. With their many prayers, unconditional love, and wisdom, we emerged from our sorrow and mourning.

During that time God told me that as long as I put Him first and train my kids to know God, then He promised He would always provide for us.

"Therefore, take these words of mine into your heart and soul. Bind them on your arm as a sign, and let them be as a pendant on your forehead. Teach them to your children, speaking of them when you are at home and when you are

away, when you lie down and when you get up, and write them on the doorposts of your houses and on your gates, so that as long as the heavens are above the earth, you and your children may live on in the land which the Lord swore to your ancestors he would give them." Deuteronomy 11:18-21; New American Bible

Unexpectedly, my dad tragically passed away from a head injury on my parent's 48th wedding anniversary. We were absolutely devastated!

My dad had sold the house quicker than he thought, right before he died, and unbeknownst to him, left us all momentarily without a home to live in.

God, I had yelled at the top of my lungs while banging on my steering wheel. **Help me!** This is too much for me to handle! I am husbandless, fatherless, and now a homeless mother of FIVE children.

I wanted something or someone to take the pain away. I felt like dying. In tears, I visited my pastor and cried out for help. He and his wife miraculously had a whole living area in their basement available for us. (Another family had moved out just the month before.) While living with my pastors, God healed our hearts in unspeakable ways. And even though I didn't have a husband or father to help provide for us, I had trust in God that He would be that for me.

As I chose to embrace my suffering and not run from it, God's Divine Grace collided with my human desperation causing me and my children to arise from our despair. This taught us how to dance upon life's tragedies.

As I was scrolling down Facebook one day, HOW TO WRITE YOUR STORY by Kary Oberbrunner caught my eye. I immediately shared it on my page and watched the webinar, thinking that this might be a way I could earn an income, but most importantly, I wanted to help other women heal and be over-comers.

Every word in that webinar resonated with me. Without even thinking, I submitted my application.

Kary interviewed me and accepted me into Author Academy Elite. After I signed the papers, I thought to myself, "What did I just do? I have no money to pay for this. Who am I to think I could ever write a book?"

Since I decided to take the plunge, God provided all the final payments for Author Academy Elite. This too was a miracle since I had a very limited budget.

Even though we still had disappointments and writing a book was a very difficult process, I can honestly say that through it all, the acute pain was far greater than the chronic pain.

We now own our own home, and my children all love Jesus and are thriving! We really are living a fearless life, full of freedom and joy.

Erica could have remained in the place she was, yet she felt compelled to do more, to bring healing to those who find themselves unexpectedly in the pit she went through. Out of the depth of pain, you have the ability to help others. Erica made the decision to step out of her comfort zone for the sole purpose of helping others.

You can decide to leave the Port of **Comfort** and impact others, yet you must intentionally pull up your anchor.

PORT 4: Growth

Growth is the ability to seek learning and gain understanding to move upward. This port is where individual lives begin to transform for those who seek to move past the door of comfort.

"I want to grow. I want to be better. You grow.
We all grow. We're made to grow.
You either evolve or you disappear."

Tupac Shakar

Growth Starts with Learning

Learning plays a big role in this port since those who choose to enter, seek a desire for growth in this state, are continuous learners. You have the ability to enter this port by deciding to make an impact in your life and to become a learner again.

After my unexpected event of being fired, I made a decision to work on myself and begin to grow within. This type of work on self is called Personal Growth. Given I was suffering inside, I saw a book in window called *Purpose Driven Life* by Rick Warren and made the decision to see what was inside this book, thinking that it could help me. That book started my pathway toward personal development.

Funny since I was not an avid reader or didn't invest time in reading much after graduation, given that I was anchored to the port of comfort. I told myself the lie that I don't have time, yet during that event I found time, and today, I work on reading a personal growth book once a month. The Statistic Brain Research Institute states 42% of college students never read another book after they graduate.[1] Before the event, I was part of that number.

Do Not Worry About Having Immediate Results

When you invest time into your personal growth, you must not be concerned if you are not seeing immediate results. You should be focused on watering the seeds to sprout growth and realize that growth may take months or even years to flourish. This port is one of impact, and you will be rewarded internally by reaching this stage in your life.

During this port in your life, you should decide to become an avid learner, a person who seeks knowledge. You should read books on personal development, or listen to audios while driving, or attend events that help you grow personally and professionally.

Seek out ways from those who are experts in their field to help you grow, so that you may achieve. But more importantly, foster your growth so you can make a greater contribution.

Learning is a personal choice. In the **Learning** Port, you were mandated or put in situations to learn. However, in this port you choose what you will learn.

Endless Resources in Today's Online World

Social media and online resources can be helpful. Most of it is available for free! You can seek out YouTube videos that provide value to help you grow. There are podcasts you can listen to daily, which provide insights to help in your business, job, or personal life. Also, Ted Talks, which provide valuable content from leading thought leaders in eighteen minutes or less.

In the waves of life each day, those in this port find time to learn. They make it a priority to feed their mind with knowledge. Those in the comfort port choose not to make it a priority, and thus never advance to this port. Although this statement is a cliché, it is still true, "Leaders are Readers." Leaders in all areas of life stay on top of their field by continuous learning.

Continuous Learning

You can decide to elevate learning in your life today and begin a journey of continued learning. There are books upon books, whether you prefer reading with a Kindle, listening to an audio, or holding a book in your hands, you can enter a subject in your favorite web browser search box and there will be many books from which to choose.

Finding something to read is not hard, but deciding and making the commitment to infuse applicable learning into your mind can be hard. Learning can also be accomplished through working with someone. If you are working on accomplishing something you have never done before, the road is easier if you find someone you can emulate.

If you seek, you will find the learning you so desire. Continuous learning is a choice, and those who reach this port in life seek knowledge and seek to take what they learn, apply, and experience growth. So, do you believe you can reach this port of growth?

PORT 5: Contribution

Contribution means helping something or someone advance. This port is for the bold who want to create a legacy and contribute to the greater community.

You may think this port is only for the wealthy, or only for those who can make a significant impact. However, do not let yourself fall in the trap of that mindset. You have contribution within you!

You—yes you—have the ability to create your own legacy and make a contribution. And after you decide you do want to create a legacy, you must understand what it is that will allow you to do that. For some, it may mean starting their own business or allocating time to help grow their favorite charity organization, or starting a foundation, or doing something they have dreamed about but did not fully know how to realize it. It can simply mean volunteering.

Contribution Can Be Volunteering

One thing I truly enjoy doing is volunteering at my church in the children's ministry. Every odd month on Sunday mornings, I read a story to the K-4 kids. Have you ever read a story to a group of kids? You need to be prepared for anything. When you ask questions, their minds are full with responses and sometimes are not aligned to the question. Yet, I still say, "Thanks for sharing!" When I prepare for the lesson, even though I've heard the story I'm sharing before, I always learn something new I can apply within my life. For those who decide to be within this port, while you are contributing, know you will also be growing.

Shift the Focus to Others

This port is moved away from the focus of "me" and "comfort" and is about "How can I add value to those around me?" This shift to focusing on others is where true contribution and legacy begins. If contribution and adding value is what you truly care about, the final port will be important to you. Helping others is what you strive for in this port, and there are several ways you can make a contribution.

Perhaps you have been on the receiving end of an organization and you want to give back. Or you have a special group that is close to your heart. Regardless of what it is, you must find the individual or group you would like to impact. Many people think the only way to contribute is by giving financially, and while this does help, you can contribute by simply giving some of your time to the cause, individual, or organization.

What is Your Legacy?

No matter how busy you may be, you can find time to invest in knowledge that will provide benefits to you and help you make your contribution to this world. Allow yourself to dream, to wonder and ask, "What will my legacy be?" You can begin now to move into this port and etch your contribution into the world, to feel the sense of value and purpose. Don't wait until your journey is coming to the end of life before asking this question, "What do I want those to remember me most about at my funeral?"

Nelson Mandela took a stand against Apartheid and fought for the equality of individuals in South Africa. His work against the government belief system allowed him to be accused of sabotage, and thus he received life imprisonment in 1964. His first day of imprisonment started on June 11 and he was released 26 years later on February 11, 1990. Four years later, Nelson Mandela was inaugurated as South Africa's first democratically elected President.

Nelson believed in mankind and having equality for individuals so everyone could live together in harmony. He believed and acted in that philosophy despite the odds against him, which created his legacy. Even while in prison for a length of time, he still kept that belief. His legacy still remains to this day.

What Port Are You in Right Now?

If you are in the contribution port, do you feel you are doing everything possible to learn and deepen your legacy to those you provide value?

If you find yourself in other ports, know you can move through each port by taking action. You can settle for the comfort of mediocrity or pursue your dreams by living an extraordinary life that provides benefits to others.

Are you ready to create your legacy?

"There is no passion to be found playing small – in settling for a life that is less than the one you are capable of living."

Nelson Mandela

Key Points

- The ports are places you get to, which you get to decide.
- Learning provides the foundation to move forward in life.
- The individual who solely focuses on themselves may seem serving to them, yet it is not serving to others.
- The port of Comfort is for those who dare not to pursue their dreams.
- Continuous learning is the gateway to personal growth.
- Contribution is not focused on your individual needs; it is focused with the intention of advancement.
- Legacy is the result of purposeful intention with the desire for impact.

PART 3
PREPARING FOR
THE JOURNEY

CHAPTER 8
THE WAVE OF COMMITMENT
THE STRENGTH OF YOUR WIND

What is one commitment you have that has lost its wind? You know, the commitment you made and suddenly over time, it lost its strength and the wind is gone.

Commitment is the act of making a claim or statement that will help you begin something and maintain a level of stamina to see it through to completion, long after the excitement of starting has worn off.

Every year, millions of people make a New Year's resolution on the first of January to get into shape, so they sign up for a gym membership or begin attending consistently. If you attend the gym regularly you have seen this. In January, the parking lots are jammed, and you have to wait for a spot to open. Once you get inside, the machines and weights are in full use, and you have to wait in line for your turn.

The Big Drop Off

However, something happens as the month of February rolls in—the previous order is restored. You find a parking space, you do not have to wait for a machine or bench, and your allocated time to work out is reduced. I read a post by Fitness Coach Darren Beattie, and he stated that 80% of the New Year's resolution crowd drops off by the second week in February.[1]

The level of commitment was initially very high for the New Year's Resolution crowd, but then something happens. The commitment level drops, and then ultimately, most people in this crowd stop going. This illustrates the difference between a fad and commitment. The individuals who joined the gyms in January and then stopped going did not make a commitment, they just rode the fad. They joined the "right thing to do" crowd and were never fully committed.

What is something you started that would make a difference if you fully committed?

"Opportunity is missed by most people because it wears overalls and looks like work."

Thomas Edison

No Alignment to Vision Stops Commitment

Once the results didn't occur in the timeframe they allocated for themselves, they told themselves, "See it doesn't work," and simply gave up and moved on. When you lack specificity with no alignment to your vision, there is a high probability you stop doing what you said you would do. This type of action is an interest.

"There's a difference between interest and commitment. When you're interested in doing something, you do it only when it's convenient. When you're committed to something, you accept no excuses; only results."

Kenneth Blanchard

Habits Will Impact Your Commitment

Habits are an indicator of your commitment. Another reason you can fall out of commitment is your personal habits. Are your habits aligned to the commitment you made? Continuing with the gym example, say you joined a gym to lose weight. You work out and decide not to change your food intake, and consequently you did not lose the weight you desired. Since you did not see any results, you stop. All of your habits must be aligned to the commitment and to the vision of who you want to become.

Even when you deploy the best habits toward your commitment, failure may still appear.

When failure does arise, it can set you back and seems defeating. For some, failure leads those to quitting, given that what they tried did not work. Patience and tenacity were not aligned with their vision. Always remember that failure will be part of the process in any level of commitment. The key to continuing in commitment is changing your mindset and looking at failure as progress, and part of the process for growth or achievement is known as "Failing Forward!"

The Shift

One way to shift your mindset when failure does arise is to journal all of the things that went well and the progress made. Let's imagine your weight loss commitment didn't meet your goal. Instead of focusing on the unmet goal, focus on the progress made and write down what actions did you take to accomplish what you did achieve. Visual pictures are also a good reminder of progress, if charting a weight loss goal. The slight change in how you perceive things is the gap between failing forward and failing, which can stop your progress.

Five Reasons Commitments Are Lost
1. Lack of vision
2. Not being willing to pursue with full engagement toward the goal
3. Not adjusting habits
4. Seeing failure as the end
5. Limiting beliefs which hold you back

My Own Limiting Belief Which Held Me Back

Not long ago, just prior to the arrival of my daughter, I enjoyed going to the gym and exercising after work. My friend Jeff and I spoke about working out in the mornings, and I recall telling him it just was not possible for me to get up and work out early in the morning like he did. We laughed and had a great discussion. I had this limiting belief that I could not work out in the morning.

One day I decided to try it. Yes, I decided to wake up early, around 5 AM, and exercised before work. My body was in total shock, and the voices in my head were saying, "What are you doing? You do not work out in the morning. You need more rest to have a better workout."

I completed the workout and went through my day, but around 1:30 PM I hit the wall. I really wanted to take a nap. Were the voices in my head correct? Maybe I did need more sleep, maybe my body was not made for working out in the morning and I should just continue what I have always done.

Overcoming Limiting Beliefs with Action

I decided it was just one day and I should try again, so that is what I did. I have been working out in the morning for over five years now and I LOVE it. I made the commitment to try to do something I really did not want to do in the first place, based upon my limiting beliefs I had about myself. But I made a decision and took action. While painful at first, I created new habits and these habits have turned into the norm. The best way to overcome failure is to keep going.

When I embarked on this new workout time, I told myself failure was not an option. I wanted to see if I could adjust my body to wake up early and go to the gym in the morning, so I could spend time with my family after work.

My new morning routine would not have occurred unless I truly committed to my goal and had that rooted desire to make it work. I could have easily snoozed the alarm and told myself I can go to the gym after work or that I can go tomorrow, and the cycle of not doing the action is then repeated, to create the habit, I had to stay on track toward my commitment.

What limiting beliefs do you have that are causing you not to commit? Spend time thinking about those things which you believe about yourself, that are causing you to delay being committed. The inner voices in your mind can derail you from accomplishing great things. You do not deserve that.

An Example of Impressive Commitment

Most of us have seen someone who is so committed that their level of commitment impressed us. Nothing stopped the individual, and they did something amazing. In my own life, there is one such individual who immediately comes to mind—Darci, who is a sitter for my daughter. She made a decision to lose weight, and not just a few pounds. She wanted to lose over 100 lbs without having any type of operation. She wanted to lose weight by doing it the "hard way," that is, through nutrition and fitness. Her level of focus and dedication was simply amazing. Watching her along her path was impressive. That level of commitment just does not happen. There are several things you must do to have that unwavering focus, that laser of attention, and to function at that level. And, yes, she exceeded her goal and is an inspiration to many people. Darci shared this with me.

Today I have lost 122lbs and I feel great! I decided to take action given I wanted to get healthy. I wanted to have the ability to run around without feeling tired. I wanted to feel better.

I setup monthly goals for my weight loss. I wanted to lose over 100lbs and I just focused on breaking that down into smaller goals every month. I would give myself little rewards when I achieved the goal. I didn't give myself any food rewards. It was rewards like a new nail polish.

While I was pushing myself to lose the weight, I must be honest and tell you there were times I was afraid of failing. There were times I just wanted to be done with the weight loss, done with eating healthy. But I did something, which triggered my mind when those thoughts entered in. I would look at a picture of me before I started the weight loss and I looked at a picture of me at that moment and saw the weight loss achieved. That keeps me going.

I would have some friends that would say, 'You've lost enough weight' or 'Come with us to this place for a meal.' I would look at the pictures and have the ability to tell them "no," or 'I'm continuing my weight loss plan.'

I knew that to lose over 100lbs I had to change my habits. I recalled before I started this, I detested vegetables. I never ate or rarely ate vegetables. My mom would have to make a special dish that didn't contain vegetables just for me. Today, I love vegetables. Instead of snacking on candy, I snack on fruit and vegetables. I eat asparagus and Brussel sprouts now! The one thing that made me stick with the commitment was, I wanted to feel happy. I would look at my pre-weight loss pictures and I could see in the pictures I wasn't happy. I had low confidence. Seeing myself this way wasn't me, it wasn't who I wanted to be.

Before my weight loss, with my lack of self-confidence I was super shy. Now having lost 122lbs, I have so much more confidence. I would never be the first one to engage in a conversation. With the confidence I have now, I was the one to engage in a conversation with a guy, who is now my fiancé and we are getting married this May.

I reached out and received the support of family and friends for encouragement and often would talk with them to receive support. It truly helped.

I feel great and am super grateful for what I have accomplished and look forward to the future with my fiancé.

Darci made a commitment, a commitment that didn't waver, and she pressed on toward the goal. Losing 122 lbs doesn't happen by accident; it was full engagement with intention and discipline. She owned her agenda! You can see her before and current pictures in the Appendix.

You possess the ability to grow beyond your current level and it all begins with owning your agenda. I love what Marie Forleo, life coach, author, motivational speaker and web TV host says,

"Be the author of your day!"

Increasing your level of commitment starts with controlling your day and taking ownership of your agenda. You can tell yourself "I do not have time," which is a limiting belief.

I am a firm believer that you can find time to do what you feel is important. There are so many distractions around you that can throw you off your agenda. For example, social media is a large distraction. Yes, it is powerful since it is in real time, but it can control your life if you allow it.

Owning Your Agenda

Similar to being disciplined about working out in the morning, I had to become disciplined about social media to complete this book. I put it on my agenda as a limited activity, and I did not allow it to be a distraction. You can do the same. If you need time to be on social media each day, schedule it. Communicate with your co-workers, family members, whomever may be affected, and let them know you are limiting your time on social media. Owning your agenda is a step of improving your level of commitment.

Understand the Values Gained Behind the Commitment

When you make a commitment, understand why you decided to make that commitment. What is the underlying story behind why you wanted to make the commitment? This is the second insight that can help you stay on your commitment road.

Your *why* must have an intrinsic or extrinsic value associated with it. Intrinsic relates to an internal reward you will receive, such as peace, joy, and happiness, for example. Darci's intrinsic value was that she wanted more happiness and self-confidence. Extrinsic relates to something on the outside; it could be financial, health, a reward received, anything which holds a tangible weight to you. Once you identify each of these values, write it down. Your commitment has meaning and it begins to resonate within your mind.

When I began my morning workouts, the intrinsic value I'd receive was more happiness since I got to be home with my daughter after work, and my extrinsic value was increased family time. If I continued to go to the gym after work, I would have had less time with her and I would feel guilty not being able to spend family time. Understanding your values will keep you aligned to your commitments.

7 Levels to Reach the Core Why

Last year, I participated in a course by Dean Graziosi called the "The Winning State of Mind" in which he discussed a 7 *Level Deep* exercise to get at your core reason for doing something.

Uncovering the core foundation of *why*, along with understanding your intrinsic and extrinsic values, will strengthen your level of commitment and keep you on your path. To find out how to obtain your core *why*, visit cardiffdhall.com/resource.

Tell Someone About Your Commitment

When you make a commitment, you need to make it known to those around you and especially to someone who will keep you accountable. Stating your commitment out loud holds a different meaning. Have you ever had an idea in your head and not taken any action on it? Now, think about a time when you told a friend or perhaps make a statement on social media about something you would do. Stating it publicly holds a heavier weight, and there is a sense of obligation you feel when you make a commitment in the universe. When I had the idea for writing a book it was only in my mind. I kept telling myself that I needed to begin, and yet I delayed action until I told my wife and my good friend Greg, and then made a public post on Facebook. Making these pronouncements made it real, and so I just dug in and began. After I shared my commitment with others, I felt accountable, which helped to keep me on track.

Having an accountability partner can offer encouragement, feedback, belief, and can help curtail limiting beliefs you hold. I have a group of AP's (accountability partners) and I gain energy, guidance, and feel their belief, which helps power me through the commitment made. When you make a commitment have an AP or group of AP's!

"Your accountability partner keeps you on track and moving forward in all aspects of your development."

Mike Staver

What idea have you been holding in your mind? Your level of commitment increases when you have that individual or team who believes in you and wants you to achieve your goal. Tell someone about it or find a group that will provide support and make the decision to get started. Good ideas do not take true flight until you make it known verbally and surround yourself with those who can support you.

Benefiting Others Can Motivate Your Commitment

When you remain committed, others can benefit; being committed also affects other areas of your life. My friend Darci was committed to losing weight and helping herself. She was helping her future and also helping others. Her commitment influenced her habits, her agenda, and the environment around her, which helped move her forward toward the goal. Yes, she was the one doing the work, but the impact of her achievement in losing weight inspired others and is giving them hope.

If you have a sense of those whom you are influencing and helping, this will motivate you to continue on your quest to remain committed. When you make that commitment, it should be aligned with your vision.

Not only is Darci providing inspiration and hope, another benefit is that she can be healthy for her family by not having health or weight-related issues.

The Personal Decision

Being committed is woven in you making a personal decision, the kind of decision that runs deep in your soul and that would make the average person say, "That's too much work," or "Why are you working so hard?" Your personal decision must be attached to your vision and where you want to go in your life. It is who you want to become. A personal decision has the mantra, "I will continue despite what comes my way."

Take Ownership

You are the captain of your ship, and by making that decision, you have taken ownership and responsibility for yourself and your life. If you watch sports or play sports you may have heard this phrase, "They have skin in the game." The individual or individuals on the team are committed. They have taken personal ownership for the outcome of their game.

Personal decision = Personal ownership

What commitments are you making to get your "own skin in the game"?

I Will Do What It Takes

Within you there must be this resiliency like a buoy that continues to stays upright and does not sink. There must be an attitude of "I will do what it takes." If you have that attitude, you have made a personal decision and have accepted personal ownership to be committed.

Imagine you are walking on the beach, and a stranger asks you to come aboard his private boat and watch over the boat for a few hours. You are delighted and feel this sense of personal ownership. The stranger could have chosen anyone, yet he chose you.

You have a personal stake since you have made a commitment to the stranger and feel obligated to watch the boat for a few hours. The same can happen when you make a commitment to yourself or someone. If you have the attitude, "I will do what it takes," you become the owner of your commitment. Being committed is a choice. It is a decision you make to stick with something until you see it through, regardless of what you may encounter. Is it hard? That depends on what you say to yourself.

Your Personal Words Impact Commitment

The words you use can either help you stay in the tracks of commitment or they can sabotage you. **Choose your words carefully once you made that commitment.** Words such as, "It's too hard", "I can't", or "I don't see myself" all create this wall between you and your commitment, and over time, will sabotage your commitment. Your choices of words are powerful. Become an active listener of what you say.

Obstacles Will Help Build Confidence

Know that when you depart on your commitment there will be obstacles that'll come your way. They are not there to stop your commitment. They are there to help build and shape your confidence, which will power your commitment.

Imagine you decide to put a little pressure on a buoy and you release it. What happens? The buoy pops back up. This time, you put more pressure on it and you release your hands. What happens? Yes, it comes back up again. This is what an obstacle can feel like. They can press down on you and you decide whether you will come back or not.

"It's not whether you get knocked down, it's whether you get up."

Vince Lombardi

When you encounter obstacles to your commitments and you overcome them, you are building resistance. You have a greater capacity to overcome even greater obstacles. This is true with anything you stick with over time.

Take Control of Your Time

You control what you spend your time on, and being committed to something takes time and needs to be woven into your daily life. Find the time to be committed, to engage in something that will propel you through your journey.

I know if you truly allow yourself to be committed, you will have accomplished more than you could imagine. Stay on the road of commitment, it will lead you places.

Key Points

- Commitments are often made at specific times of the year, yet fail to be aligned with a vision or bigger purpose.
- Habits are a predictor of your commitment.
- Your limiting beliefs will hold your back from making a commitment. Those limiting beliefs can be unchained by action.
- There must be an intrinsic or extrinsic value associated with your commitment.
- Surround yourself with AP's who will support you to build your belief and confidence.
- Accept personal ownership and decide to anchor your mindset in "I will do what it takes."
- Your commitment will encounter obstacles, and if you allow it, your vision will be the tug boat to pull you through.

CHAPTER 9
THE WAVE OF YOUR POD

INFLUENCES

Take a moment to think about the circle of friends with whom you spend time with, and write down the answers to these questions.

- What activities you do share with them?
- What ideas do you share together?
- What jobs do your friends have?
- What vacations do your friends go on?
- What things do you typically discuss?
- What range of income do your friends have?

You might be saying to yourself, "Who would care about the type of income my friends make? Isn't that snobbish?" Well it is, if you think so. The purpose of this exercise is for you to do a self-evaluation and take inventory of the people with whom you associate.

"You are the average of the five people you spend the most time with."

Jim Rhone

Stop and think about that and allow it to anchor within your mind. Through the circle of life, we go through a series of friendships that will create our future.

To best illustrate this, let us look at your high school friends. High school, when I was growing up, was all about the "group" you were in. What group? The group of friends you hung around with before, during, and after school.

- What did your friends do?
- What did you have in common with them?
- What activities did you do?
- What grades did your friends get?

If you are true to yourself, you will most likely see that somehow, you were well matched with your group of friends. Is this bad? Well, you can decide that for yourself. Perhaps your group missed classes and did not take school seriously. Perhaps your group was involved in sports, school activities, or made the dean's list. Your friends influenced your activities in high school and the same holds true in adult life. It has been said, "Birds of a feather flock together."

Be Prepared to Be Pulled Back

After you take inventory of your pod, you may decide you need to adjust your circle of friends to move forward in your journey. This can be difficult and you should be prepared for negative comments. I am reminded of the story about the crab bucket.

One time a man was walking along the beach and saw another man fishing in the surf with a bait bucket beside him. As he drew closer, he saw that the bait bucket had no lid and had live crabs inside.

"Why don't you cover your bait bucket so the crabs won't escape?" he asked.
"You don't understand," the man replied. "If there is one crab in the bucket it would surely crawl out very quickly. However, when there are many crabs in the bucket, if one tries to crawl up the side, the others grab hold of it and pull it back down so that it will share the same fate as the rest of them." [1]

If someone is trying to leave a group, the other members may try to pull that person back, and if they cannot pull him or her back, there may be negative actions by the group. This can include making comments about that person. When you decide to leave the pod, it is known your desires are not aligned with the group's desires anymore.

Let's imagine you meet with a group at least once a week to just get together and talk about...well, you can't remember. Your meet-ups are that memorable. You begin missing the local weekly night gatherings because you start attending a weekly online training in the evening instead, or decide to do something to improve yourself.

There will be resistance from your group, especially when you consistently miss the meet-ups. You have chosen to do something that is outside of the circle of the pod.

Remember, your circle of friends may not be on the same path as you, so don't believe you should feel guilty about not attending. After several weeks, expect the pod to do what it can to get you back. Just know you are now doing something they may not understand and you have to be ok with that. You are developing a new circle of friends, and these new friends share the same desire to improve themselves.

Choose Friends that Are Supportive

Some friends will lift you up and believe in you. Some friends will grab at you just like the crabs to bring you back. Which groups of friends would you pick, if you desire to do something that you believe in? No question, you would want those friends who support you, who believe in you, and who will help you achieve what you desire.

If you recall, my friend Darci found a group of friends who offered her support and increased her belief. She would connect with them for encouragement and would lean on her group to push her through times of difficulties. These types of friends empower you and build you up!

Don't fall into the trap of thinking, "I cannot find friends who will support me." That thinking is not true. You can find someone to support you. That person could be a trainer, a speaker, or a thought leader in his or her profession. Darren Hardy comes to mind. Do I know Darren personally? Not yet; however, I subscribe to his Darren Daily emails and I receive insights from him during the week, which help me. I share Darren just as an example of the individuals with whom you can connect via the internet. You can connect to Darren Daily at www.darrendaily.com.

Moving On from Non-Supportive Friends

If you have a friend who is not supportive and you truly aspire to move forward and achieve something, moving on is only difficult if you allow it to be. You have the choice, not that person. You can be discreet and just stop being around this person or you can talk to them.

Here is something you could say, "I have appreciated our friendship, and although there are some things which we do not agree, I still value you as a friend. I recently started something that will require me to focus on reaching new goals within my life, and will require a great deal of my time and energy. I have to do this for me and I am sorry if it means we will have less time together."

You have to decide on what you want to accomplish within your vision, and it might be worth losing friends in order to gain friends who will believe and support you. Only you can decide.

Share Your Vision – Some Could Be Supportive

I am not saying do not ever talk to these old friends again, of course I'm not. Perhaps some of your friends begin to notice how you are changing and give you a compliment, wanting to know more about what you are doing. That is great, and you should share with them and help them understand your vision and where you want to go. Hopefully, they will be supportive of you.

Select Your Friends Wisely

Friends will either stop you from achieving your vision, what you desire, or friends will help support you and provide the "fuel" that is needed to bring your vision into formation. I would rather have friends that are providing "fuel" rather than using my "fuel" and emptying my tank. Select your friends wisely, and remember, you are the average of your five friends.

"A friend is someone who understands your past, believes in your future, and accepts you just the way you are."

Unknown

Key Points

- Friends will either keep you from departing on your journey or be there alongside your journey.
- Consider your five closest friends and do a self-evaluation.
- The right friends will provide encouragement and increase your self-belief.
- Look for support outside of your current circle and be willing to connect with them.
- Decide to distance yourself away from friends who are not supportive of your journey.
- Realize your vision can be fueled by the right friends.
- The journey with the right friends will allow forward movement or they will keep you docked with them.

CHAPTER 10
THE WAVE OF YOUR GPS

SHAPE YOUR MINDSET

Mindset is the collection of substance that is built with habits, internal infusion along with action and then relayed to your brain, which then can influence the outcome of a situation. The substance is the attitude you feel toward what you are working on. Mindset is something that builds over time, and you can direct how much or how little to create.

Mindset is the mental energy that gives you the best opportunity to achieve success. If your mental energy is empty, you will never achieve what you so desire. Before you engage in a task, project, or business, it starts between your ears. That is truly where it begins, which sets the stage if you can achieve or not.

"I truly believe in positive synergy, that your positive mindset gives you a more hopeful outlook, and belief that you can do something great means you will do something great."

Russell Wilson

Create the Right Mindset

I want you to imagine you are going to enter a single person rowing race and you've always wanted to row in a big event. You've done the rowing device at your local gym and liked it so much, you decide to find a rowing club to join. You have been on small rowing events and have done well, however, the race you are entering is longer in length and the waters are a bit unstable.

You tell yourself rowing should not be that bad since you already know how to row. You mentally do not prepare because of what you told yourself, and thus do not spend too much time training. You feel prepared given you've done other rowing events. You are excited for the day, but when you start, what you heard about the waters is true and you struggle right at the beginning.

You somehow continue to row, but your heart feels like it is about to erupt so you stop rowing. Frustration has set in, so you head over to the edge and drop out of the race. Do you see that by just telling yourself that you knew already how to row it did not prepare you adequately, thereby affecting everything you did?

Your mindset, in a sense, predicted your outcome. What you fill your mind with will create the substance that will either propel you forward or keep you from accomplishing.

Don't Let Others Stop You

Creating the right mindset can help you achieve, even if those around you do not believe you can do it. Many people allow other people's thinking to penetrate their mind, and it destroys the level of their thinking and sabotages them.

You cannot allow other people's negative thinking to influence you or stop your progress. I read a story about a lawyer who had a successful corporate career and was on track to become a partner. While in the process of trying to become a partner, he was moving away from who he was, so he decided to go in a different direction by leaving the company and going out in his own business.

His peers said he could not do it. They said he would fail. However, they underestimated his mindset. He left the company and created his own successful company, demonstrating that having the right mindset can block out the naysayers.

The Right Mindset Is a Protective Shield

The right mindset can power you through any obstacle or challenge. It is a protective shield, and when someone throws something at you, with the right mindset, this will bounce off you. Developing that type of mindset is critical. I love how Roger Clemens states how mindset can help you.

"I think anything is possible if you have the mindset and the will and desire to do it and put the time in."

Roger Clemens

Affirmations Can Help You

Developing the type of mindset where you do not get thrown off course starts with you. There are a few ways to begin to develop and improve your mindset. The use of affirmations, which are short phrases that take a limiting belief, turns it positive and pairs it with the sense of vision, having accomplished what you are affirming.

Imagine you do not enjoy speaking in front of groups, small or large, while your job function requires you to do so.

An affirmation to help with your ability to speak in front of people could sound something like this: "I am so happy and grateful that I have the ability to easily speak in front of groups." Telling yourself this out loud allows your mind to begin to work to find a solution to do just that.

Write your affirmations on index cards and read them out loud, twice a day. Read them when you get up and when you shut off the lights to go to sleep. While you are sleeping, your subconscious mind will absorb the last thing you put into it.

If you travel for work, you can create a folder or a photo album on your phone of the affirmations to read while you are in hotels. Affirmations help you develop your mindset, and your limiting beliefs will begin to fade way.

I have used affirmations to help bring this book to life. I had a self-limiting belief that I did not have time to write a book, nor did I believe I was an author. Here are two affirmations I used to build my internal belief system.

"I am so happy and grateful I have found time in my daily schedule to write this book, which God put in my mind."

"I am so happy and grateful I am a published author."

By focusing on these two affirmations twice per day, they began to seep into my mind and built my protective shield, allowing the self-limiting beliefs to dissipate.

Along with affirmations such as "I am," you can also create affirmations such as "I used to believe I could not _____, but now I am getting better at _____." These type of psychological mental hacks can break the anchor holding your limiting belief. Now take a few minutes to write out your limiting beliefs.

On the three lines below, write down what limiting beliefs you have, professional or personal.

1. _____

2. _____

3. _____

Now write down the affirmation that takes your limiting belief and turns it into something positive. Affirm accomplishment and improvement in your affirmation. Start the affirmation again with "I am so happy and grateful" or "I used to believe _____, but now I am getting better at _____."

1. _____

2. _____

3. _____

State Your Affirmations Out Loud

Take the time to develop three affirmations that focus on your limiting beliefs. When you read them, it is imperative you truly BELIEVE what you are telling yourself, even if you do not know how it will come to completion. Do not worry about that yet. Just allow your mind to work for you. Your job is to simply BELIEVE your affirmations and read them out loud twice a day. Take this seriously, and do what the average person is not doing. You are building a better **YOU**!

What You Say Shapes Your Mindset

Another way to help build your mindset is with the language that you use or think. Below is a list of 10 words/

phrases that show limiting beliefs. Circle or make a note to yourself when you say these words aloud or think them.

1. "I can't"
2. "I don't know how"
3. "No one will support me"
4. "Should have"
5. "Could have"
6. "Would have"
7. "I don't have the skills"
8. "That's not possible"
9. "I am not good at..."
10. "I can't see myself doing that"

Did you score a 10 out of 10, or 5 out of 10? Whatever your score, you can change what you say immediately. What you think or say has an impact on you and your ability to do or not do something, and it directly affects your mindset.

"It's not what you say out of your mouth that determines your life, it's what you whisper to yourself that has the most power!"

Robert Kiyosaki

My Own Limiting Words Used

When I had the idea to write this book, I was using all sorts of words and phrases that were self-sabotaging. Words such as, "Who I am to write a book?", "I can't find the time", "I don't know how to do this." These were just a few. All of these were stopping my progress before I began drafting out the chapters. Do you see how these words and phrases can stop you before you even get started? To change this language, I started filling my mind with positive energy, reading great books and listening to mentors such as Brendon Burchard and Les Brown. Filling my mind with positive vibrations and words helped depress the limiting words I used.

Affirm Your Future with Positive Words

Saying the right words over time will either propel you into action or keep the engine silent. If you use the right language and believe in yourself when others may doubt you that can be enough to move forward. Saying the right things to yourself provides the right fuel and it is up to you to take the repeated action necessary to achieve your vision.

Another way to help with saying the right words and to help fuel your belief is to transform a negative statement into a question. For example, instead of the phrases listed above such as, "I can't", "I don't know how", "I can't find any support", ask yourself these questions: "How can I?", "How can I learn the skills?", and "Who can support me?"

The Power of Words

Take the time to transform your negative phrases and turn them into a question, and allow your mind to work and find a solution. That is the power of words that you use. While you are out in a social setting, pay close attention to what you say and what others say, and see if you hear any words that are limiting.

Know that you create and control the words and statements you use. When you find yourself making limiting statements, just flip it around and ask that statement in a question. This will help improve your mindset.

Self-Development Defined

Self-development is the act of acquiring knowledge to help you grow into the person you desire to become. I must be honest with you and tell you that just a few years ago, I did not engage in self-development, or used the "I do not have time" mantra that so many people use, and I found myself in the comfort stage.

While looking back on it, I knew I was not growing. Yet I did have a desire to do more and create a personal legacy. One day, I made the commitment to get serious about personal development. Now I am acquiring knowledge, which is shaping me and allowing me to grow into the person that God put on this earth, to impact others. When I made the commitment, I found time to invest in myself.

Self-development is an investment in yourself, which helps your mindset grow. Similar to a garden or your lawn, when you want to ensure that you have the best flowers or the greenest lawn, you use fertilizer as the agent to help you achieve that goal.

Focus on Self-Development, Build Your Book Library

There are different ways you can develop your mindset through self-development. One way is to find a book on a topic you would like to know more about, and then read the book. I want to be clear and say that self-development books generally are not written as works of fiction. You need to find the right books that will provide substance to help you along your journey of life. I have created a list of recommended books that I included in Appendix B.

I travel frequently, so now I read on flights. I am always curious to look around and see what others are reading to see if I should add another book to my reading list. I recall sitting next to an individual from Wisconsin on a flight from Minneapolis to San Diego and he was reading a book about connections with daughters. We had a great conversation about the book and he was so kind, he sent a copy to me.

If you hear about a good self-development book write the title down. I have a massive list of books that are on my list to read, and I want you to have your own massive list. Reading books and implementing some of the keys from these books can change your life. Reading without implementation of a key point made in the book is not getting the true value of the book. Yes, it helps shape your mind, and there must be practical application in your life for you to see and feel the benefit of what you have consumed mentally.

"The more you read, the more you know; and the more you know, the smarter you grow."

Jim Trelease

Connect with Mentors

Another way to develop your mindset is to connect with a mentor. This can be done meeting one on one, connecting with a mentor online such as blog post or social media outlets, or with presentations and meetings.

Having a mentor you meet with locally, or someone you follow online, can provide insights and help you become more than you are. It will help build up your mindset.

Get to know how he or she thinks, what advice they have and see how they can help you. Often their content is free. All you need to do is find that individual, listen, read, and apply.

Attending the Right Events Can Build Your Mindset

Another way to continue to build your mindset is attending events. Not the kind of events that are meant for entertainment, but the type of events that are meant for teaching something. I had the opportunity to attend an event where I heard Zig Zigler speak. WOW!! He was amazing, and I was happy I had invested time to attend that event.

When you attend an event dedicated to self-improvement, you will be in a crowd of like-minded people. You will be with people who seek achievement or want to improve in some way. Do not look at an event as "another waste of my time" or make a judgment that "those people are too happy" or say "I do not have time to attend those things" or "I do not have the money." These develop limiting beliefs.

If you find yourself saying something like this or these types of statements, then you are living in a fixed mindset, which is blocking your ability to grow and achieve. You are also in the self-sabotage mode when you use such phrases. Events are held in many cities around the world, and all you need to do is find an event that speaks to you and make the decision to attend.

I attended a Brendon Burchard event titled High Performance Academy, which helped me expand my performance. Today I am sustaining more energy without having to rely on coffee or other liquid boosters. I rely on the natural booster of getting a minimum of seven hours of sleep to provide the energy required. Attending this event also expanded my belief, mindset, and vision.

Infuse A Daily Routine to Build Your Mindset

Developing a mindset is not a one-time affair. It is a daily routine that, over time, will become a habit. Every day you eat some types of foods that provide the energy your body needs. The same applies here. You need to work on developing your mindset every day by doing any one of the suggested ways to increase it. Decide to allocate an amount of time every day to developing your mindset. I suggest you infuse at least 20 minutes per day.

Or if you are not doing anything today to work on your mindset, then allocate at least a few minutes. Start with 5 minutes and keep adding every day until you have invested at least 20 minutes per day. If you do this, you will invest 2.3 hours per week, and over a year you will invest 121.7 hours in mindset training! Imagine what you can achieve if you do this. So make the time to invest in yourself and build your mindset, so you can achieve your vision.

I was recently mentored by a coach who has developed an incredible mindset, and below are his insights on how mindset can help you achieve.

First off, Cardiff Hall has been absolutely incredible. He's literally been the most coachable individual I have ever run across. We met at Top Earner, Ray Higdon's annual event in June 2014. Like I talk about all the time, mindset is the number one thing you must have in order to succeed. Do not worry; I can prove this to you.

How else can people that have less than you, less skills, less money, and less time, still exceed in their business or opportunity?

You see, if you believe you can make it happen, you will. If you believe that you cannot make it happen, you will not make it happen. Mindset is not something you do once. It is kind of like bathing. You have got to do it day in and day out. You see, somebody with a very solid mindset cannot be budged; they cannot be influenced by anybody they do not want to be influenced by. If your mindset is right and it is rock solid, you will start to attract the things in your life you need to succeed. We all think it is about the how-to's and those are generally the products that we buy, but what gets us from point A to point B is mindset. Because if you think you can do something at a super high level you will crush it. It is just a matter of time. My wish for you is you adopt this philosophy. You have got to believe that in mindset and how much you believe in yourself makes a difference. You have to believe you are worth *it. You have to believe you are worthy of success. You have to believe you are worth pouring energy and time into. I am here to tell you I believe in you and you are worthy of success.*
Terry Gremaux

Increasing your mindset will increase your success. Decide to take daily steps to create the fuel you need to enable your mindset to grow and you can move forward in your vision.

Key Points

- Your mindset can positively or negatively impact the level of success or lack of success.
- Having the right mindset will shield you from negativity, which blocks your path toward achievement.
- Ownership of your mindset starts with you; the habits and strategies you use can build or tear down your mindset.
- Affirmations help reduce and eliminate self-limiting beliefs, which hold you back from reaching achievement.
- The words you think and say are the direction of your mindset.
- Your mindset is shaped by who you can become, which can occur in the process of self- development.
- Daily infusion of building your mindset will propel you forward toward your vision.

CHAPTER 11
THE WAVE OF HBF

UNDERSTAND YOUR INTERNAL ENGINE

D o you know your HBF score? Imagine someone walks up to you and says, "Can I ask you a question?" You say, "Sure," and next you hear, "What is your HBF score?" You repeat back to this person, "My HBF score?" with a slight doggone look on your face, and the person responds, "Yes, what is your HBF score?"

You actually think about it and respond, "Do you mean credit score?" And the person says, "No, your HBF score." You honestly have no idea what the person is referring to so you simply blurt out "100!" and the individual looks at you now with a doggone look back and tells you the scale is 0-10 and just leaves in bewilderment.

Everyone living has a HBF score and that score changes during your life. It helps you access your level of performance. Okay, I know you are asking, "So, what is this score that everyone has?"

HBF stands for **Hope, Belief, and Faith**

Low, Medium or High HBF

Your HBF is a selected number on the scale of 0-10. A HBF score of 0-4 represents Low HBF, a score of 5-7 represents Medium HBF, and a score of 8-10 represent High HBF.

You have individual scores for your relationships, your job, your future, and your finances and so on. Your HBF score is ultimately one score that drives everything you do. Take out something to write with and think about what range your hope, belief, and faith would fall into: Low, Medium, or High, and write down that number. That number provides a benchmark of how you perceive yourself, and I will help you explore these levels.

Before I discuss the levels, it is important to define what exactly are Hope, Belief, and Faith.

Hope

Perhaps you have heard that hope is a crutch, something you cannot rely on. However, that simply is not true. Hope can be viewed as an ingredient that is used for mixing, which if combined with other ingredients provides the foundation for you to move forward to achieve. Hope is something that is not seen, but is a way of thinking that starts internally. You cannot buy hope at the grocery store or at your favorite hardware store.

Hope starts inside you and must continue to build, if you want to achieve. Hope can provide the strength for you to continue. Louis Zamperini, US Olympian and WWII veteran who survived 47 days in a raft after his plane went down in the Pacific Ocean, lived and said this about Hope.

"Hope provides the power of the soul to endure."

To build your Hope, you must find that value within yourself; it can be intrinsic or extrinsic. There is an underlying reason for Hope and that lies within you. If you have set your vision, Hope is tethered to it. For those without a vision, your level of Hope is often wavering, given there is no set direction but merely drifting along in life.

You can also build Hope by being around others who have achieved in what you have yet to accomplish. Having a platform upon which to stand on will build up the level within you.

Everyone has the same opportunity to generate the same amount of Hope, yet it is those who are purposeful about setting the course for their vision, building up the highest levels within themselves, who succeed.

Belief

Belief is the unwavering substance that controls the mind to confidently feel that things will work out. The substance is something that cannot be physically touched, because it resides in you. How much Belief you have may be based upon what you have experienced along your journey in life so far. If your road has been easy, your Belief could be high. If your road has been difficult, your Belief could be low.

Belief is a word that you may associate with your past; however, Belief can also be focused on the future, that which is unseen. When you drive a vehicle every day, you observe the gas level. There is even a light or warning signal to remind you the level is low and you need gas to continue going. Think of this tank in a similar way regarding your Belief. When your Belief is full, there is nothing to deter you from achieving. At this level you express positive energy and your outward appearance probably includes having a smile on your face!

What happens when your Belief level is low? If your level is low, you will not be able to achieve. You will be unable to even move forward. You feel helpless or unmotivated. Your energy changes and you become stagnant.

But you have the power to decide where your level of Belief is. Just because your tank is full of Belief, it does not mean it will not go down. It will go down, just like your vehicle's tank gas level will go down, and if you do not stop and fill it up, it will run out.

How to Increase Your Belief

The way to fill your Belief tank is by feeding positive energy to your mind such as:

- Reading uplifting books
- Getting mentored by a coach
- Being connected to a group
- Volunteering

All you need to do is to be aware when you are low on Belief and take action to fill your mind back up.

Faith

"Faith is the confidence that what we hope for will actually happen; it gives us assurance about things we cannot see."

Hebrews 11:1; New Living Translation

Faith is concerned with that which is unknown or what is yet to become. Having Faith requires having a deep confidence from within yourself. Its presence within you is greater than you and can help set and direct your goals and dreams, regardless of not fully knowing how it will turn out. Faith does not happen overnight. It comes from what you tell yourself and what occurs in your mind. Faith requires a certain understanding that you do not have all the answers, or that you may not know exactly how something will be done. But you know deep within you that somehow you will figure it out.

There are a few ways you can build your Faith. Remember, it begins with the input into your mind and the things that you are telling yourself.

First, do not allow yourself to say negative things such as, "I don't know how. I can't. I have never done it." All of these statements are not delivering Faith input into your mind. Second, you must have a vision and have the ability to see yourself already accomplishing a task or goal. Finally, get around others who will support you. If you do all three of these simple things, you will begin to build your Faith by the strong inputs into the mind.

A quote from an unknown author sums it up this way.

"Faith is taking the first step even when you cannot see the whole staircase."

HBF Scores

You now have an understanding of the meaning of HBF and how all three qualities together provide the foundation for you to achieve. Having an HBF score of 0-4 is low and this level is not serving you, if you want any level of success or achievement. With this score, your Hope, Belief, and Faith are essentially nonexistent. At this level, you may blame others for where you are and you may not look at life as rewarding, but rather as a job that you do not like to do.

Negative events in your life may have created mental scars that have limited your ability to recover and move past the events. While your hope could be low, your belief could be a bit higher. But if your faith were also low, this would create an overall low score.

If two of the three HBF ingredients are low, you have a score in a low range. Reach out to individuals you admire, or mentors who help can move your HBF score up.

If you have a score of 5-7, your HBF is medium. Your Hope, Belief, and Faith level could all be equal in nature, not too high or too low. This is where the majority of people exist. They have good levels of all three ingredients but have doubts that creep in such as fear, which holds them back and reduces their HBF score.

For those of you who have an HBF score in the medium range, make sure your vision is clearly defined. Plotting the course first then ensuring what you are doing fits with your personal vision will bolster your HBF score. If you align everything back to your vision and work on setting the right mindset to increase your Hope, Belief, and Faith, you will be able to increase your score and transition to the next higher level.

High HBF Score, Foundation to Your Success

Having an HBF score of 8-10 is where you need to be to operate and reach your full potential. In this range, all ingredients of your HBF score are high. Your Hope, Belief, and Faith are so strong, that it gives you the ability to achieve what you are seeking. This level is what some refer to as "high performance." You want to reach that level within you, so you can reach your own "high performance."

Once you move along your own personal HBF scale and achieve a high level, it is possible you may slip back down the scale. However, the dip will not last long, if your mindset has been powered effectively with positive fuel for your mind.

"A positive mind finds a way it can be done; a negative mind looks for all the ways it can't be done."

Napoleon Hill

Refuel Your Mind

Again, think of your HBF score as a high performance boat. What does the captain do when the boat is running on empty? Stops and refuels. If you notice yourself sliding back down the scale after reaching a higher HBF score, there are a few things you can do to refuel.

Go back to your vision and renew it. Plug into one of your favorite authors or leaders, and read or listen to their words. Lastly, talk with a mentor or someone close who inspires you. These are simply ways to get that quick shot of fuel you need until you are back at operating at a high HBF level! You can continuously operate at this level; it is just a matter of choosing to allow your mind to go there.

Keep Your HBF Score High

Gathering more of each ingredient in your HBF score is a choice you make every day. When it may seem like things are not going right, you may slip to a level of thinking and say, "Why is this happening to me?" Your HBF score drops with that way of thinking. Instead, when things appear not to be going well, say to yourself, "What can I learn from this? How can this help me?" This statement can immediately increase your HBF score and allow you to focus on what is possible.

Wherever you are on the HBF scale, know you can adjust your score since it is fluid and not fixed. Only you can control the power to direct your score.

The chart below represents the level of performance associated with your HBF score. Decide to operate at level of high performance to accomplish what you desire in your life.

HBF Bell Curve

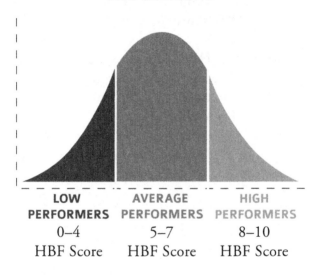

LOW PERFORMERS	AVERAGE PERFORMERS	HIGH PERFORMERS
0–4	5–7	8–10
HBF Score	HBF Score	HBF Score

Source of Graph: VPD Consulting[1]

Key Points

- Your HBF is your internal engine, which provides the source of power to achieve.
- Hope is not a crutch; it is the essence built within the mind.
- You can set your belief level while others can influence it; it is you who controls the inputs.
- Faith requires you to believe in the unknown.
- Your HBF score is a contributor to your performance.
- Realize your HBF score can slide up or down and you have the ability to change it.
- Take the necessary actions required to develop a high HBF and allow your vision to guide you.

PART 4: STAYING ON COURSE

Chapter 12
The Wave of Confidence

Develop the Foundation

C onfidence is the unseen substance that resides within one's self, which is the spark in believing you have the capability to do something. Confidence may permeate your being, or it may be trapped. Everyone has it, and the life you have lived thus far has conditioned your confidence. The good news is, you can build or repair it, if it is undeveloped or has been damaged.

Build Confidence Over the Long Term

Although your confidence may waver daily, your confidence wave may be going up in a positive slope. It should show that, over time, you are gaining greater ability to accomplish things. Confidence will dictate whether you achieve your dreams and goals, or whether you are impeded along your journey.

Marcus Garvey, the Jamaican political leader who grew up in the early 1900s, had this to say about confidence.

"If you have no confidence in self,
you are twice defeated in the race of life."

You must have the unseen substance of confidence if you desire to achieve.

The First Test of Confidence

Do you remember taking those first steps to walk? You might not. You raised yourself, steadied yourself, and took that wobbly step and fell down. Then you did it again and fell, and did it again until you were able to keep your legs steady. You might have not known it then, but you were building confidence every time you tried to walk, fell, and got back up.

Confidence Can Increase or Decrease

You go through experiences during your life that shape your confidence. The level of confidence you have today is associated with your "wins." If you have tried something and you have succeeded, then your confidence increases. If you failed or things did not work out the way you designed, your confidence decreases. The more someone struggles, the more often they have less confidence.

Look at the struggle as a confidence-increasing opportunity, instead of as a confidence-decreasing activity. Allow the grips of failure to build your confidence instead of deflating your potential.

Thoughts Impact Confidence

In all of your experiences, if you focus on the negative things and what did not work, your negative thoughts will diminish your confidence. However, if you focus on one thing that was positive during the negative outcome, you are silently building your confidence. Although it may not feel like you are building your confidence immediately, your positive thoughts will influence your confidence in the long run.

Those with Whom You Associate Can Impact Your Confidence

While experiences and thoughts impact your confidence, those with whom you associate also impact your confidence. Imagine starting a small business in an industry you are not in today, and you have had this idea for some time. You begin to share your idea but your circle of influence tells you, "You can't do that. You don't know anything about that." Such statements can diminish your confidence and stop you from launching your idea.

Now, say your circle of influence tells you, "That is awesome, I know you can do it" or "You can accomplish anything." These statements give you more confidence. Since they are positive, they give you energy that helps build your confidence. Your close associates can build or take away your confidence. The circle of association is a choice you have.

When I began the outlining chapters to the book and I mentioned this idea to my own circle of influence, the majority of them mentioned positive comments. Of course you will run into those who may not share your same vision, and I did hear comments such as, "Do you know how to publish a book?" or "Do you know how to write a book?", and "You don't have time." I chose to listen to the positive comments shared with me and not focus any time thinking about the opposite comments. I understood they didn't share the same vision as me and that was ok. I was not going to allow the misunderstood comments derail my journey.

*"Someone else's opinion of you does not
have to become your reality."*

Les Brown

Being around a group that believes in you will push your confidence higher. I became a member of an author group called Author Academy Elite, run by Kary Oberbrunner. This group of authors is an inspiring group who cheers each other on, who believes in each other and shares success ideas to bring value and benefit to everyone in the group. The group does not believe in scarcity; it believes in abundance. Having a group of like-minded individuals will push your confidence level up, like this group has done for me.

The 4 Cs of Confidence

In the course I invested in by Dean Graziosi called the "Winning State of Mind," he shares his 4 Cs of Confidence, which are Courage, Commitment, Capabilities, and Confidence.

The 1st C Is Courage

Courage is the ability to move away from your area of comfort. If you are willing to face your fears and do something that stretches you, your courage will build your confidence. Courage is about taking action; it is not living in the "Someday Syndrome."

Do you find yourself saying "Someday"? Why?

- Are you afraid of failure?
- Are you unsure of how to start?
- Are you concerned that you may not have the skills?

Every person on Earth has courage. It is up to you if you use it or not. What passion or idea do you have that is sitting on the shelves collecting dust?

One who has limiting beliefs is unable to do something. It is how we think that creates the ability to have courage and take action.

My Courageous Action that Paid Off

Courage is the adhesive you need to build your confidence. In the early 90s, while I was on vacation, I had the courage to ask a lady who I did not know if she wanted to dance. She said, "No." I then immediately stated to her, "I am on vacation, **come on** dance with me." I believe she was just doing me a favor so she could get rid of me. I guess I was wrong! We are celebrating 20 **years** of marriage this year! If I did not have the courage to simply ask her a question and then follow up with a statement, the course of our lives would be different.

You probably remember a time when you took some action that required courage, and it probably felt uncomfortable at first. If you continue to have courage and face the uncomfortable situations, you will increase your confidence regardless of the outcome.

The 2ⁿᵈ C Is Commitment

Commitment is the act of taking action. It is drawing a line in the sand, pushing your chips all in, and making that statement of commitment. By committing to taking action, you automatically build confidence. You must be willing to move forward without knowing if you will achieve or not. Those who choose to wait so they can increase their probability of achieving never truly win and never truly achieve.

Lack of Action Can Impact

Where I grew up there was a video rental outlet called Blockbuster. They were a provider of home movie and video game rentals, and at the peak of their business in 2004 had over 9,000 stores. There were two smaller companies on the rise called Netflix and Redbox. You probably have heard of them. These companies contributed to Blockbuster going out of business. In my opinion, Blockbuster could be around today. They chose not to make the commitment to move quickly into the direction of Netflix and Redbox. Instead, they simply waited to see if this new trend would take hold. That lack of commitment led to the closure of the company.

THE 3rd C IS CAPABILITIES

Think of capabilities like tools within a toolbox. When embarking on something you have never accomplished before, you need to have the right tools to help you achieve. It sounds simple; however, many rush off to accomplish something without gathering the tools they need to help them succeed.

The more capabilities you have, the more you will build your confidence. Your tools could be a coach or mentor, books, audios, a group, friends, and materials you need. While there can be a number of different tools you have at your disposal, engage in using the tools that can help you. Similar to a boat builder using tools, a variety of tools are there to help you. You must stay open to learning and developing skills that will enable you to continue to achieve.

*"Achieving your dreams means facing the
reality of your capabilities and limitations."*

Unknown

If you understand what you need to advance and then
secure the tools you need, you can overcome your limitations with your capabilities.

The 4ᵗʰ C Is Confidence

This is a mindset you must have to achieve.
I love Dean Graziosi's quote.

*"When you follow what everyone else does,
you get what everyone else has."*

You must think differently and it begins in your mind.
What you think about expands in your life. If you think
you cannot do something, your mind goes to work and
proves you right. If you decide to tell yourself you can,
your mind will begin to work on figuring out how you
can do it.

Your mind is a powerful engine, and what you feed
your engine determines how powerful or weak your mind
will be. Be aware of what you are feeding your mind daily.
Here are several things you should be watchful of, which
shape your confidence.

Avoid Negative Information

Today, negative information sells ratings. It is every-
where, and it infiltrates your mind consciously and sub-
consciously, weakening your mindset and reducing your
confidence. When I tell people I have removed myself
from the news they look at me in a funny way. I have

heard some people say, "That's not American." But often the news is unhealthy and I choose not to feed my mind on unhealthy subjects.

If you have never done a news media cleanse, I suggest you try it for 30 days. Stay away from news on TV and radio. This includes local radio, because even local radio includes negative news. Instead, use that time to listen to a great audio book and learn something.

Negative TV programming along with negative based movies will also influence your level of confidence. Feed your mind the right food, so your mindset can deliver the confidence you want to achieve.

Watch Out for Bad Advice

In addition to the news, there are other external things that will lower your confidence. Be aware of bad advice you are getting. Imagine wanting to train for a marathon and you ask a co-worker for some tips. They have not even completed a 5K race yet, but then they give you so many tips that you get lost and don't know what you should focus on first. That is bad advice and will weaken your confidence.

It is best to seek input from someone who is accomplished, someone who has run at least one or better yet, several marathons. This will help build your confidence.

Avoid Focusing on Your Weaknesses

Another factor that can lower your confidence is focusing on your weaknesses. By focusing on the "bad" thoughts about yourself, it feeds your subconscious mind, which confirms how you feel. If you put 100% of your focus on your weaknesses, this will destroy your confidence. No matter what level of confidence you have today, you can increase that level by doing those things that reinforce your confidence, instead of focusing on your weaknesses.

Beware of Social Media Influences on Your Mind

Today, social media permeates all of our lives. Simply scrolling through feeds on Twitter or Facebook can positively or negatively influence your mindset, and it can build up or break down your confidence. Use your time wisely in deciding which social media feeds to spend time absorbing in your mind.

There are other factors that can help build your confidence.

Establish Good Habits

Along with infusing the right things into your mind, you can also increase your confidence by establishing good habits. Your habits help develop your confidence. Imagine if you wanted to go on that dream cruise vacation and you made a plan to save a certain amount monthly to pay for the trip. The habit you need to begin is saving money today, so you are rewarded in the future. You decide each payday to move funds to another bank, just for the sole purpose of taking your dream vacation.

The first month goes by and you make a deposit. Then the second month, you follow through by making another deposit. Each month you are able to put more into the bank, and every time you invested in your vacation, your confidence improved. You know your dream cruise vacation will happen. You developed the habits that gave you more confidence.

Write Down Your Monthly Goals

Setting goals is a great way to help build your confidence. Write down your goals for each month. These are short goals that can help you stay on track for that month. These goals can be targeted toward family, recreation, job, finances, or a project; it just requires that you take time and write them down.

Many people avoid writing down their goals because they think that just having them in their head will be good enough. I was one of those individuals while in the comfort stage. I thought just mentally knowing my goals would be enough.

If you do that, life and other priorities get ahead of the things you put in your mind, and guess what happens? Yes, the goals you have in your mind are lost. They just disappear. If you have not written down your goals for the month, just take some time right now and use a pen to write down, "What do I want to complete for the time remaining this month?" Write what comes to mind then repeat it at the beginning of every month after.

Written Goal Process

Underneath each goal you write down, include how you can achieve the goal and when you will achieve it. The more specific details you can add to your goals, the more you will increase the possibility you can accomplish them.

Be Willing to Sacrifice

During the summer of 1987—sounds like a song title—I made a commitment to sacrifice something. I decided to try out for the Ohio State University marching band and attend summer practice sessions, which were optional on Tuesday and Thursday evenings. The sacrifice I made was spending less times with my friends. The summer after high school graduation was about fun, spending time with friends before leaving for college.

That summer, instead of spending my free time with them, I chose to spend the majority of my time practicing, attending the optional sessions, which required me to drive 90 minutes each way from my hometown to Columbus, Ohio. It was great to have a good friend, who was also trying out for the band, join me on these weekly trips to Ohio State.

My sacrifice paid off when I heard my name called that late August night before the start of Labor Day. My name and position in the band was announced; I had made it! My friend also made the band. The college football season was a week away and I would be playing on the field on Saturday afternoon, not in a football uniform, but in the Pride of the Ohio State Buckeyes, The Ohio State University Marching Band.

A commitment will require a level of sacrifice—trading something today to receive something of value on the other side of your commitment.

Take Action Avoid Delay

I see many people wait for everything to be just perfect before they take action. Waiting can cause you to move away from confidence. And the further you move away from confidence, the worse you feel. You begin to blame. You begin to say life is not fair. You say, "It is not my fault." Do not allow yourself to fall into the sea of delay.

Taking action may be hard at first after making the initial commitment. Decide you will move away from that sea of delay and simply take action, so you can increase your confidence.

"The path to success is to take massive, determined action."

Anthony Robbins

Confidence can flow like the tides of the ocean. If you implement the strategies in the chapter, you will increase your level of confidence and move toward the achievement you so desire.

Key Points

- Your confidence is fluid and will increase or decrease along the journey you have embarked on.
- Thoughts, while silent, can be the anchor that just drops thus halting your progress.
- Those who provide input to you should be carefully vetted and taken in, if it pushes you toward your destination.
- Positive groups can be the wind that enables you to continue the path forward.
- The more courage you generate, the greater level of confidence you build.
- Influences to the mind will increase or decrease your level of confidence.
- The path to move forward must be met with a clear vision, sacrifice, set goals, and initiated action.

CHAPTER 13
THE WAVE OF INNER STRENGTH

DISCOVER YOUR WILL

Inner strength is the will, the determination, and the drive to proceed, to continue. It is the substance in your body you cannot physically touch or see.

Sports Showcase Inner Strength

If you watch sports, you have seen events that have showcased this in an individual or team—such as the individual runner who is in last place but in the final moments of the race finds a gear and blazes by the other athletes to win the race; or the runner who stumbles and falls, and then wins the race. Or the team that is behind several scores and appears to have lost the game, but then begins to score, gain momentum, and finally find a way to win the game.

Sports are filled with stories of inner strength. What makes an individual or team have that inner strength? How does a team go from almost losing to winning the game? How can one person stumble and fall and win the race? You can say luck, or that he or she or the team just got lucky. That's the type of response that is made by the unbelieving, those who do not understand the process of building inner strength.

Inner Strength Can Be Built

Where is your inner strength today?

You have inner strength; in fact, everyone does. It is a matter of choice if you choose to build it or allow it to remain dormant.

If you have young children, what occurs when their favorite toy does not work? You probably took out the old batteries and inserted new batteries so it could work. The toy did not work because the batteries were dead. The toy was dormant. The same applies in your life. Everyone possesses inner strength, but your batteries may be dead.

The good news is that you can decide if you want to create the energy needed to increase your level of inner strength. I know you want to, since you are reading this book so you can move ahead in your journey.

To perform at a higher level, you need a higher level of inner strength.

Those in the comfort stage avoid doing so, because increasing their inner strength requires a four-letter word and that is called WORK. This is the biggest difference that separates those who utilize their inner strength and achieve high performance to those who do not.

"Strength does not come from physical capacity.
It comes from an indomitable will."

Mahatma Gandhi

An Example of Inner Strength: Dennis Kolb

I had the opportunity to meet a great young man named Dennis Kolb. George Fraser and Les Brown shared his story in the book *Mission Unstoppable*. Dennis had a fight with a type of leukemia and while receiving his chemo, he was overdosed. He shares his battle in the book about what occurred after the overdose and how he reached inside himself and garnered his inner strength.

He could have decided to focus his energy on blaming everyone involved in his care, but he chose to find that inner strength to live, to survive from something that was clearly a mistake. The choice he made has impacted his life and others. You also have the same choice, to reach for that inner strength despite the circumstances or outcome.

The average wants to know the outcome before they decide, if they should do the work required. This type of mindset is not aligned to generating any energy. Did Dennis know the outcome? No, but he chose to have faith and believe his inner strength could pull him from the brink of death. Wherever you are currently along in your journey or situation, you need to have a mindset of possibility and make the decision to connect with, and develop, your inner strength.

Dennis built his confidence and did not look at obstacles as the dead end, but rather reached for that inner strength. To surpass whatever in life was put along his journey. You can also do the same.

Some choose to accept life the way it is while some decide to expand and utilize their inner strength to work toward a goal. You can use your inner strength, and there is a way to build it so that when you want to reach for it, your tank is full.

Ways to Build Your Inner Strength

There are several things you can do to increase your inner strength, which will help your mindset. You must get around the right people. Earlier, you went through

Wave of Your Pod, so you should now understand that who you spend time with will influence everything you do and the way you think. You want to spend time with individuals who provide energy, as opposed to those who take away your energy.

Do you believe that if Dennis had individuals around him who were so focused on blaming and wanting revenge it would have helped him get through his leukemia? No, that would not have provided any help. Make the decision to be around those who can build your mindset

To continue to maximize your inner strength, continue to put good things in your mind.

The Mobile University

You can utilize the mobile university to build your inner strength. I do this daily. If you do not use the mobile university, decide to put it into practice. Instead of listening to the radio or news while driving your vehicle, listen to a podcast, book on CD, something uplifting to help fuel your mind. Think about the amount of time you spend in your vehicle and how that time can improve your inner strength.

Vision Fuels

To continue to build your inner strength, you must know where you want to go and understand that there will be difficulties along the way. Knowing where you want to go is about your vision. If you know which way you are pointed and are doing those things to move you along in that direction, you build your inner strength.

Imagine a circle and another circle within that circle, and another one within, continuing until there is a small dot in the middle. The dot in the middle represents your inner strength. The further away you are from the dot, the harder it will be for you to feel that inner strength to help push you along. Having that vision will fuel you to move toward your inner strength.

Spiritual Emotional Connectivity

Building your inner strength requires a higher level of belief and faith. There is something that can provide the power you're unable to generate yourself. That source is God.

"Now all glory to God, who is able, through his mighty power at work within us, to accomplish infinitely more than we might ask or think."

Ephesians 3:20; New Living Translation

There is a story from the Bible about David who went to fight Goliath the Giant. David believed he could conquer Goliath by tapping into the inner strength from God, and he did. You can do the same. You can connect spiritually and ask for wisdom, guidance, and inner strength to help you.

You can simply say to yourself this short prayer.

"God, I ask for your guidance and wisdom in what I am doing, give me the strength to get through this, so I may achieve."

Allow your heart to connect with your mind when you reach out for guidance. I trust you will engage in this higher level of belief and faith. Allow it to supply the inner strength to achieve.

Acquiring inner strength does not mean you will accomplish and achieve in everything you do. Life is not that way. During failure, you can still build your inner strength by continuing, by not giving up, by making the declaration of "**I will persist until...**"

Failure builds your inner strength but only if you continue, which is a choice. Understand the ways to tap into your inner strength, which will build up over time, and then you will experience that blast that can push you over the line of achievement.

Key Points

- Inner strength is the will and determination to succeed.
- Your inner strength can be built over time, which is a personal choice.
- Obstacles can be overcome when your inner strength is strong.
- Filling your mind with positive emotional content will help increase your level of inner strength.
- The closer you are to the core of your inner strength, the more it will give you the ability to move along in your journey.
- It requires a greater level of faith and belief to be connected to the ultimate source of inner strength, God.
- Forward progress will require your level of inner strength to be full and unwavering.

CHAPTER 14
THE WAVE OF VICTORY

YOUR NAUTICAL MILES ARE WORTH IT

Victory is a word you hear when an individual or team wins a championship, a gold medal, or a race. Don't be fooled into thinking that victory only applies to teams or those in a sports professional role. Victory is available for more than just a team; it's available for you!

Perhaps you have self-limiting beliefs such as, "If I win, that would not be fair" or "I do not deserve to win" or "When I do win, it will just bring me more issues." You may have self-limiting beliefs about winning, which will constrict any advancement to your Victory Island.

Every person has the ability to win and create victory for him or herself. Let me define victory so we can develop an understanding of how to win and what is needed for you to reach Victory Island.

Victory is the end result of a continuous effort put forth to achieve something that will provide benefit to your life. You determine the benefit. You decide what that benefit is and what value it provides you.

"Victory belongs to those that believe in it the most and believe in it the longest."

Randall Wallace

Victory starts with the belief you have inside of YOU. The starting point is the point at which you make the decision to embark for something that you aspire to achieve. You may look at your life and say to yourself, "I have not truly won at anything." Do not get caught in the net associating victory with a valued item such as a prize or money.

Victory can be intangible or tangible.

Something tangible, for instance, is this book. You took action, made a decision to purchase, and have the ability to read something that can help you.

Six Masts Needed To Reach Your Victory Island

Mast are the tall poles that sails hang from on a ship.[1] To reach your Victory Island you must have these six masts embodied within you, so you can move forward along your path toward achievement. These six masts are the activators that will give your sails the ability to extend while on your journey.

1. **Belief in your best self.** Believe in your abilities and know you can achieve!

2. **Spend time visualizing.** Take 15 minutes every day to close your eyes and see yourself as already having achieved your goal. Feel the positive emotions associated with the achievement of your goal.

3. **Commit to excellence.** Be committed to doing those things that will propel you forward at your best ability. Excellence occurs after continuous effort.

4. **Be resilient.** Resilience is required when you set off toward your Victory Island.

5. **Be accountable**. Hold yourself to a higher standard and take responsibility for everything along your journey.
6. **Be positive**. Have you ever heard or seen an individual who did not have a positive attitude achieve something great? Be positive and be around those who radiate positivity each and every day. Being positive will allow the momentum to continue moving forward.

The journey along the path to Victory Island is one of ups and downs. If you charted the course for those who have reached Victory Island, you would see a course with ebbs and flows that may look like jagged peaks and valleys, but in the meantime, there is forward progress. It is in those valleys where you will be tested and your mast will stand tall, allowing you to continue sailing.

Victory and achievement await those who take command of their ship and seek to move forward every day.

Key Points

- You have the ability to reach your own Victory Island.
- Victory can be seen as tangible or intangible.
- Achievement is for those who believe in their best self.
- Hoisting your six masts will enable forward progress.
- Commitment to excellence will propel you forward.
- Spend time around those who are positive so it powers your momentum.
- Be the captain of your ship and take command of the miles traveled along your way to victory.

CHAPTER 15
THE WAVE OF SUSTAINING
YOUR WINDS

HOIST YOUR SAIL WITH ASSURANCE

You made it through the waves and you have reached Victory Island, which is fantastic!

Now what? You feel great about what you have accomplished and perhaps have set your sights on another goal. Just because you have achieved victory and success does not mean you will do it again.

Yes, I know that sounds harsh but it is true, unless you do certain things to ensure you will reach Victory Island again. If you look at the Super Bowl Champions, it is rare to see the same team win the Super Bowl in consecutive football seasons. Currently, there are only 7 NFL teams out of 32 teams that have won consecutive Super bowls (Green Bay Packers, Miami Dolphins, Pittsburgh Steelers, San Francisco 49ers, Dallas Cowboys, Denver Broncos and the New England Patriots).[1]

> *"The ultimate definition of success
> is the ability to repeat it."*
>
> Jeffrey Benjamin

There are seven steps you need to do, to ensure you put yourself in the best position to reach your next Victory Island.

1. **Avoid success paralysis.** Overconfidence is a major symptom of success paralysis, and you can become complacent and believe you can take short cuts since you have already achieved once. In success paralysis, you lose the hunger and power necessary to move forward.

2. **Ensure habits are reinstated.** It is easy to let your habits slide after you've achieved something, but you must realize it is the daily principles that shaped you and kept you on course.

3. **Avoid living in the glory of victory.** Yes, celebrate your accomplishments and spend time reflecting on what you achieved. Do not keep floating in the clouds months after you made that achievement. The victory celebrations should not be prolonged. They should be limited.

4. **Avoid listening to what is being said about you.** Do not allow the things said about your accomplishment and victories go to your head and cause you to stop your momentum. You see this in sports, where an individual will have success and they allow what is being said about them to halt all progress forward until soon they become irrelevant in their sport. Be appreciative of what is being said, but do not wallow in it.

5. **Set a plan to get back into action.** You see professional sports athletes who have just won a tournament or event get back the next day into their mode of operation.

6. **Avoid false belief.** Avoid believing that just because you achieved victory, it will be easy to reach the next Victory Island. This false belief can impact your habits, mental toughness, and your desire. Do not fall into this false belief trap.

7. **Review what you could have done better.** Ask specific questions of yourself in all areas along your journey to victory such as, "What could I have done better?" Write it down and develop a plan to improve with learning. Improvement is fundamental in the journey to sustained achievement.

"Success is never final. Failure is never fatal.
It's the courage that counts."

Coach John Wooden

Continuing to reach more Victory Islands along your journey of life is possible for you. It comes down to choices, your clarity, and courage. Will you persist until you reach your goal again and when you reach the next Victory Island? Will you persist again and continue your journey toward sustained achievement?

Key Points

- Achieving success one time does not guarantee you will reach your Victory Island again.
- Do not fall in the net of overconfidence in your continued journey.
- Habits define whether you move forward or stay anchored.
- Reinstate a mode of operation to continue taking advantage of your winds, which will propel you forward.
- Reflect upon your success and journal on what you can improve upon, and develop a learning plan.
- Choices, clarity, and courage will advance you toward your next Victory Island.
- Victory and success should not be a one-time occurrence; it should be a sustained process.

AFTERWORD:
VIEW FROM THE SHORE

Standing on the shore of life, you will encounter the many waves discussed in this book. How you react to each one is entirely up to you, but I trust you have a better understanding of navigating your way and reaching your own Victory Islands. You have the ability to shape the direction of your journey in life, which takes commitment, time, and sacrifice. Every person is given the same amount of time every single day, and it is the choices you make that will define and shape your journey.

You can decide to stand on the shore and watch the ocean instead of discovering what is out there. Since you are reading this book, you are not one to stand on the shore. You want to embrace life and live a life of sustained achievement.

Start with your vision and who you want to become. You have the ability to shape your life, if you have an idea of who you want to become. If you know where you want to go and you maintain that course, you can reach your destination and it begins with your vision.

There are several things discussed earlier that can help you along your path. You must have a mindset of growth and learning. The mind is powerful—it is the engine behind what powers every action you do. I shared strategies you can do to improve your mindset, and I trust you will put those into action, if you have not started already.

It is important on your journey to surround yourself with the right people, especially your top five, because of the level of influence they have in your life. Are there people in your top five with whom who you should spend less time? It may be very hard to do this, especially if it is a family member. But spending less time with them will help improve your mindset and strengthen it so that their words and action do not anchor you.

If you decide to move away from the shore and direct your life, there is something that will touch every single person in life and that is the unexpected event. You will not know when it is coming and there will be no warning. It is similar to a tidal wave.

How you respond to the unexpected event is a choice. Although the event can be hurtful, how you respond will signify how quickly your recovery takes place. Remember, you do not have to go through the event alone. There are others to help you, but you may need to reach out to someone and just ask for their help.

Sailing from the shore, you can see as far as your eyesight can see the blue ocean water horizon. This is the same for your life. You can see the weeks and months ahead, yet do not see the years nor know what will happen along your journey. Your job as captain of your boat is to guide the boat with purpose and mission.

You need to have a strong HBF. By now, you know what that means. And you have the ability to increase it by implementing the tactics shared throughout the book.

The unknown can be scary, unless you strengthen your HBF and make the decision to direct the course of your life. Your journey will be filled with peaks and valleys, similar to captains facing high seas, mechanical failures, or potential unexpected issues with the boat, which slows progress. If you continue to hoist your sails, you will reach your Victory Island, which perhaps you thought was not possible once you sailed out into the ocean of opportunities.

By developing habits and surrounding yourself with individuals who will support and help, you can achieve more than what you thought was possible. But it will require work, sacrifice, and an unwavering vision.

You can be a **TIDE TURNER** and be the captain of your ship. You are equipped to handle the challenges—which can be a ripple or a tidal wave—whichever it is, your ship is much stronger after reading this book.

On your journey, the choices you make define the direction in your life. I trust you will take several actionable insights and put them into practice. Continue to move forward with your vision and know you can impact those around you and inspire others.

You have dreams that perhaps are sitting on the bookshelf, and need to be dusted off and put into motion. But only you can do that. It does not matter where you are on your personal journey, you can change the direction IF you want to.

What is one dream you have put on your bookshelf? Write it down and list out the things or people you would need to help you accomplish that dream.

Do not put conditions on the things you need or tell yourself this person would not help. Do not fall into the net of assumptions.

Reaching Victory Island does not happen unless you make a choice and decide to put forth the effort and work to accomplish your goals. Make the decision, the choice to live a life that you want, and reach for your dreams. Believe in yourself and know that I believe in YOU!

One of my favorite songs is *You Make Me Brave* by Amanda Cook & Bethel Music. Below is part of the chorus, or you can view the video at youtu.be/6Hi-VMxT6fc

You make me brave
You call me out beyond the shore into the waves[1]

Be brave, be the captain of your ship, and face the waves along your journey toward the Islands of Victory, and you my friend will become a **TIDE TURNER!**

Appendix A

Tide Turners Resource

Tide Turners Free Resource

I have developed a Tide Turners guidebook which will reinforce the Waves discussed and bring additional understanding, so you can maintain control of your life and be the Captain of your ship. You can download the guidebook at any time at www.cardiffdhall.com/resources and enjoy the journey towards your Islands of Victory.

APPENDIX B

Recommended Books

In Chapter 10, The Wave of Your GPS, I mentioned a list of books that can help you along your journey. The books mentioned below are a few of the best among the many books I have personally read and are not listed in any particular order.

I believe sharing book titles is a great way to grow your library. You must take action by digging in and reading the book or listening to the audio version. If you love it, read or listen to it again. You will absorb more and the content will continue to help you grow. Continuing to invest in personal development will enhance your mindset.

Title	Author	Quick Link
All-Pro Wisdom	Matt Birk	http://amzn.to/2aLkrhd
Secrets of the Millionaire Mind	T. Harv Eker	http://amzn.to/2aF-1CIS
Failing Forward	John Maxwell	http://amzn.to/2aLl6zm
Think and Grow Rich	Napoleon Hill	http://amzn.to/2aLlf5O
The Motivation Manifesto	Brendon Burchard	http://amzn.to/2aLkBVQ
The Prayer of Jabez	Bruce Wilkinson	http://amzn.to/2aIKB3J
What to Say When You Talk to Your Self	Shad Helmstetter	http://amzn.to/2a-HuNLs
Don't Give Up, Don't Give in	Louis Zamperini	http://amzn.to/2aO-zyGG
The Greatest Salesman in the World	Og Mandino	http://amzn.to/2aCrXrp
Aspire	Kevin Hall	http://amzn.to/2a-HuXCt
The Slight Edge	Jeff Olson	http://amzn.to/2aCrN3k
The Energy Bus	Jon Gordon	http://amzn.to/2bb-zUYZ
The Compound Effect	Darren Hardy	http://amzn.to/2a-HufoX
Inner Voice	Russ Whitney	http://amzn.to/2aCsLwh
The Traveler's Gift	Andy Andrews	http://amzn.to/2aCsDNt

APPENDIX C

ACKNOWLEDGEMENTS

Thank you to my loving wife Dawn for putting up with me in the process of writing. When I had the idea for a book, you did not laugh and you were interested in what it was going to be about. You believed in me, and I thank you. You helped me with the initial title and provided feedback throughout the process. You told me to put my full focus and attention to see it through to completion. Without your support and love, this would have just been a dream that collected dust, and I am grateful for your push and encouragement.

Thanks to my creator, God, who inspired me with the words and gave me faith and hope when I was struggling and embarking upon my first voyage into the book publishing world.

I am grateful for my church family for believing and supporting me.

Terry Gremaux, who provided inspiration and mindset training that has helped me in the process of writing. Just connecting with you regarding our daughters was appreciated, since you had walked in my shoes and had also experienced what I was going through.

Chris D. Costello, whom I met through Facebook and is a great friend. I appreciated your words when I informed you my book was lost, destroyed along with the hard drive on my computer. You said, "Just know your book will be even better now." Thanks for your belief in me and giving me the inspiration I needed, especially when I realized I had to rewrite over 90% of the book.

Greg DeTullio, meeting you and Monica in Napa was set-up by our Creator. You believed in me and supported me along the way. Your support with texts and calls just to connect were always timely. Your humor is off the charts and we can talk for hours and laugh together. I appreciate your inspiration and for providing your belief in me.

My Buckeye friend Mark (Markus). Your story is powerful and I have seen you grow, and thus I wanted to include you in a chapter. I have appreciated our friendship from the first day we met and that has not wavered.

Thank you, Ed Ennis, Sr. While in Dallas, you took the time to talk with me and have consistently taken time out of your day to talk with me and provide suggestions. Your energy is contagious and I simply love listening to your wisdom.

Thank you, Scott Rehl, my partner. We met on my first Ignition trip and we became friends from that day forward. You listened, lifted me up, and have been there for me. Our friendship is deep and we continue to lift each other up.

Thank you, Brian Dilsheimer. Twenty plus years ago, our friendship began at a little company located in Minneapolis. You had the courage to connect with me and show me something. Honestly, although I had no idea if it would work, I trusted you. You have opened the doors and awakened my senses to personal development, and this is a result of the path you provided me.

Thank you, Jeff Meyers, my roommate in college, best man in my wedding, and simply a great friend. Although we are hours and miles apart from each other, you have found the time to connect with me. Each time we talk, it feels like time has not passed, and that is the mark of a true friendship. You give me energy, and for that I am grateful.

Thank you, Colm Geraghty. We have spent many holidays together and I was honored to be the best man in your wedding. Our friendship is similar to the words in the Ohio State alma mater, "How Firm Thy Friendship!"

Thank you, Bill Slowter. Your presence remains with me although cancer has taken you away. You took the time during your schedule to always make time for me and give me advice. Our breakfast meetings were so special and I cherish those times together. Of course watching Ohio State games together and our touchdown rituals are etched in my mind. I trust you are proud of my journey and I know your handprints are a part of this, since you helped shape my mind.

Thank you, Mark Summers. Our relationship was started from an introduction from Bill Slowter, whom I am greatly honoured. Sitting in Caribou, getting to deeply know each other, and dinners out with our wives enriched my soul. When I asked you to write the foreword, you didn't hesitate and made the commitment to be part of this journey. Your guidance and support after Bill's passing, and still to this day, remain unwavering.

Thank you to my parents (Mom and Dad). I often wondered when I was a young boy, "Why in the world did I get named Cardiff, this isn't a common name?" I know you didn't want me to be common but rather someone who stood out. You have always supported, prayed, and have been there for me throughout each chapter of my life. I am blessed to have you as strong Christian parents.

Thank you to my brother Freight Train or Uncle Choo. Appreciate your support, my man! You've always been a fan and supported me in my endeavours.

Thank you to Mikey Mikeworth. You have broadened my view and shown me what is possible. You have stretched my mind, and somehow every time we meet, my mind hurts in a great way! You have a gift and I am blessed you would share it with me.

Thank you to my editors Joan Holman and Precy Larkins. This isn't possible without you. Your skillful masterful editing has taken me on a journey and has set sail for future books. I am forever grateful for the time you've personally taken to shape and mould this.

Thank you to Krystal Lucas. Your orchestrations of the things people do not see are meaningful. I am honoured to have your assistance in bringing Inspiration Impact, LLC to life.

Thank you, Kary Oberbrunner. You are a true servant leader, and having you as my author coach, I am deeply blessed that my journey came across your path. The brilliance and program of Authors Academy Elite has aided my efforts and brought this book to life.

Members of my Advisor Board: Mark Summers, Janelle Jordan and Paul Carver. Taking time out of your day to guide, shape, and listen to me is greatly appreciated. Thanks for joining this journey with me.

NOTES

Note to The Reader

1. United States History, "Important and Famous Women in America", http://www.u-s-history.com/pages/h1551.html#1900s, accessed on April 14, 2016
2. Ibid
3. Oprah Winfrey, "Wikipedia", https://en.wikipedia.org/wiki/Oprah_Winfrey, accessed on April 14, 2016
4. University of Connecticut Women's Basketball Team, "Wikipedia", https://en.wikipedia.org/wiki/Connecticut_Huskies_women%27s_basketball, accessed on April 14, 2016
5. John Wooden, "Wikipedia", https://en.wikipedia.org/wiki/John_Wooden, accessed on April 14, 2016

Introduction

1. John C. Maxwell, *The Maxwell Daily Reader*, "Steer A Course" (Thomas Nelson, 2007), 32.

The Wave of Floating

1. Vision, Business Dictionary, http://www.business-dictionary.com/definition/vision-statement.html, accessed February 20, 2016.

The Wave of Failure

1. Babe Ruth stats, http://www.baberuth.com/stats/, accessed March 4, 2016.

The Wave of Choices

1. Robert Harrow, "Average Credit Card Debt in America: 2016 Facts & Figures", http://www.valuepenguin.com/average-credit-card-debt, accessed March 2, 2016.
2. Darren Hardy, "Darren Daily, The Compound Effect", accessed February 29, 2016.

The Wave of Habits

1. Melissa Dahl, Today, "Think it'll take 21 days to make your resolution a habit? Try Tripling that" Dr. Maxwell Martz, http://www.today.com/health/think-itll-take-21-days-make-your-resolution-habit-try-2D11826051, accessed March 5, 2016.

The Wave of Ports

1. Reading Statistics, http://www.statisticbrain.com/reading-statistics/, accessed August 8, 2016.

The Wave of Commitment

1. Percentage of new gym members in January stop coming, https://www.quora.com/What-percentage-of-new-gym-members-in-January-

stop-coming-after-February, accessed August 8, 2016.

The Wave of Your Pod

1. Andy Rodriguez, "The Story Of The Crab Bucket", http://www.abestweb.com/forums/showthread. php?8248-THE-STORY-OF-THE-CRAB-BUCKET, accessed March 20, 2016.

The Wave of HBF

1. Human Resource Management, "How To Create A Bell Curve", May 30th, 2015, http://www.hrwale. com/performance-appraisal-management/how-to-create-a-bell-curve-chart/, accessed March 28, 2016.

The Wave of Victory

1. Boat Masts, http://www.macmillandictionary.com/ us/thesaurus-category/american/parts-of-boats-and-ships, accessed August 23, 2016.

The Wave of Sustaining Your Winds

1. "List of Super Bowl Champions, *Wikipedia, https:// en.wikipedia.org/wiki/List_of_Super_Bowl_champions,* accessed April 11, 2016.

Afterward- View from the Shore

1. Amanda Cook & Bethel Music, "You Make Me Brave", https://youtu.be/6Hi-VMxT6fc, accessed April 10, 2016.

When asked, most people would describe **Cardiff D. Hall** in two distinct ways: he's got a passion for life and he's relentlessly optimistic. Cardiff has been that way for as long as he can remember, and he wants others to start feeling the same. In fact, it's become a mission of sorts.

So Cardiff tapped into his entrepreneurial spirit (*not to mention, his relentless optimism and passion for life*) to found Inspiration Insight back in 2015, with the ultimate goal of transforming lives and developing a social media platform to amplify his messages.

Through Inspiration Insight LLC., as well as his writings, speaking engagements, and personal coaching sessions, he inspires people to direct the cause of their lives rather than letting life happen to them. And in doing so, they can start living a life much like Cardiff's — one of sustained achievement.

Cardiff is a student of Brendon Burchard's High Performance Academy and has applied these learnings into his mission. He's an author within Author Academy Elite, whose founder is Kary Oberbrunner. Cardiff currently lives in the greater Minneapolis area with his wife, Dawn, and their beautiful daughter.

Connect at: Cardiffdhall.com

Belief is the hidden tool needed to scale the mountain.

~ Cardiff D. Hall

CPSIA information can be obtained
at www.ICGtesting.com
Printed in the USA
LVOW04s1147090117
520292LV00032B/861/P